MW01200255

Have you ever felt Puplava's wonderf... question and then brings you on a captivating explo... answer. Many women give of themselves, pouring out their time, energy, and resources to those they love only to wake up in mid-life and beyond feeling disconnected from their dreams, design, and purpose in Christ. This book is perfect for anyone who feels like they've lost touch with their core identity or simply wants to have a fresh perspective on life. If you're ready to embark on a journey of self-RE-discovery, *Where Did ME Go?* is an exceptional guide. Each of the 365 daily devotions will leave you with a renewed sense of purpose and hope. Warmly recommend!

—Patricia King
Author, Minister, Media Creator and Host

Where Did ME Go? will motivate you to live out your passions and fulfill your dreams. This book really encouraged me with its practical and personal insights. It caused me to look deep within myself at the real me and discover what really makes me come alive! Expect to be empowered as you ponder and reflect on the soul-searching questions at the beginning of each month. Mary Puplava will lead you on a journey to becoming all you were created to be!

—Karen Barkman
Founder and CEO, Provision of Hope

What you hold in your hands is a life message intricately woven by God. These pages not only offer invaluable encouragement and practical wisdom, but also an outpouring of love that will resonate long after you complete this reading experience. God desires to unfold this message further and reveal hidden treasures within you.

—Shell Cowper-Smith
Women's Pastor, Gathering Place Church
Certified Family Coach

Mary is a strong woman of God who abounds in wisdom and exudes the glory of the Lord through her great love. I know this book will bless and empower many women as they discover who *ME* really is! Be who you are called to be.

—Christy Pearce
Strategic Prayer Coordinator, Christian International
Santa Rosa Beach, FL

Mary Puplava is a top-notch communicator who oozes creativity with a unique blend of order and purpose. She's got her own act together and has plenty of juice to bring many of us to the top of the mountain with her. Most of all, Mary's unwavering commitment to Jesus Christ qualifies her to lead us with this volume curated for women over forty. Get ready. You will love this book.

—Shirley Weaver
Shirley Weaver Ministries
A Clear Trumpet Inc.

Mary has walked long, hard paths of caring sacrificially for others. Simultaneously, she has nurtured the need and desire to build a deeply receptive inner life with God. Enjoy her inspired, insightful guidance as she takes you to a new appreciation for who you are and who you were created to be.

—Ky Prevette
Contemplative Prayer Retreat Leader, UK
Career Missionary, Assemblies of God

Mary Puplava is a woman of God on a mission. Not only is she a wonderful intercessor and prayer warrior, but she is also a creative writer with a message for women. Her book will be a wonderful blessing to all who read it.

—Bob Maddux
Founding Pastor, Trinity Church
San Diego, CA

WHERE DID ME GO?

A One-Year Devotional to Rediscover You

MARY PUPLAVA

WHERE DID ME GO?

Scripture quotations taken from the Amplified® Bible (AMP), Copyright © 2015 by The Lockman Foundation. Used by permission. lockman.org. Scripture quotations are from the ESV®Bible (The Holy Bible, English Standard Version®), copyright© 2001 by Crossway Bibles, a publishing ministry of Good News Publishers. Used by permission. All rights reserved. Scripture quotations from The Authorized (King James) Version. Rights in the Authorized Version in the United Kingdom are vested in the Crown. Reproduced by permission of the Crown's patentee, Cambridge University Press. Scripture quotations marked (NIV) are taken from the Holy Bible, New International Version®, NIV®. Copyright © 1973, 1978, 1984, 2011 by Biblica, Inc.™ Used by permission of Zondervan. All rights reserved worldwide. www.zondervan.comThe "NIV" and "New International Version" are trademarks registered in the United States Patent and Trademark Office by Biblica, Inc.™ Scripture taken from the New King James Version®. Copyright © 1982 by Thomas Nelson. Used by permission. All rights reserved. Scripture quotations marked (NLT) are taken from the Holy Bible, New Living Translation, copyright ©1996, 2004, 2015 by Tyndale House Foundation. Used by permission of Tyndale House Publishers, a Division of Tyndale House Ministries, Carol Stream, Illinois 60188. All rights reserved. Scripture quotations marked TPT are from The Passion Translation®. Copyright © 2017, 2018, 2020 by Passion & Fire Ministries, Inc. Used by permission. All rights reserved. ThePassionTranslation.com. All scriptures marked as BSB are taken from the Berean Standard Bible. All scriptures marked as BLB are taken from the Berean Literal Bible.

ISBN Paperback: 978-1-961557-39-0

ISBN Ebook: 978-1-961557-74-1

ISBN Hardback: 978-1-961557-75-8

Library of Congress Control Number: 2024911149

Messenger Books
30 N. Gould Ste. R
Sheridan, WY 82801

Table of Contents

Dedication

For every woman who knows there's so much more to me.
God sees you, is for you, and wants you
to be all He created you to be.

A Note to My Reader

Dear Cherished Woman of God,

This one-year devotional was designed for you to begin on the first day of the new year. However, you may have purchased or received it at a later time.

It is my heart's suggestion that before you start on the current date, you read the book's introduction and at least scan the prior months. It will help you to understand the flow of becoming the *me* you were created to be.

With much love,

Mary Puplava

Introduction

When was the last time you looked in the mirror and smiled at yourself? Perhaps, like me, you thought, *Where did* me *go?*

Once we hit adulthood in our twenties and thirties, we step into the business world or start families, and we women can feel a little bit lost and forgotten. Women over forty face complex issues physically, emotionally, relationally, and spiritually. We've transitioned from adulthood and careers. However, once we hit forty and beyond, we aren't what we do. From menopause to empty nest, women who defined themselves one way now deal with what some call the invisible woman syndrome.

You pour your lives into your work and families and now care for aging parents and the younger generations. We are "The Bridge Generation," providing support for both. Expectations are high—whether you put them on yourself or others place demands on you. Somewhere along the way, you may have given up your dreams and perhaps even your true identity as the kingly and priestly daughter that God called you to be.

As you read this devotional, His Word will revive and revise you. You will rediscover who you are in Christ and how important you are to Him and His kingdom's purpose. Each month's theme will include an invitation to uncover the truth about the *me* the Father created you to be.

Reflecting on these daily Scriptures, Holy Spirit will enlighten and inspire you to receive, believe, and activate His truth in your life. You will embrace your identity and worth for His purpose as well as become more effective in praying and proclaiming declarations over yourself, your loved ones, and your world.

Arise, woman of valor. You were born for such a time as this! Transform from lamb to lioness and church attender to kingdom builder. Shake off the dust from your dreams, and see your potential and God-prepared destiny.

Who is *me*? You are a daughter of the King of kings, and the words from your mouth will be like swords cutting through self-doubt, loss, and discouragement about yourself and your circles of influence. You won't recognize yourself when you look in the mirror on December 31st. You will be the one and only *me* God uniquely created and ordained you to be.

I am your God, the living God. Wasn't I the one who broke
the strongholds over you And raised you up out of bondage?
Open your mouth with a mighty decree; I will fulfill it now,
you'll see. The words that you speak so shall it be.
Psalm 81:10, TPT

January

WHERE AM I, AND WHERE DO I WANT TO BE?

You've decorated, celebrated, and enjoyed your holidays. Normalcy returns. It's New Year's Day, so it's out with the old and in with the new. Resolutions are easy to make and break. Unfortunately, most fizzle out as your days, weeks, and months progress.

This year is going to be different. We will spend a whole year establishing your resolutions in faith with the help of the Lord, His Scripture, and your declarations. How? By starting at the beginning.

January's devotions will provide an inside look at your physical, mental, emotional, relational, and spiritual states. You need to understand where you are to rediscover the real *me* God created you to be. Each day will close with an honest prayer and a simple declaration. Say them out loud. Repeat the declaration throughout your day. Create an atmosphere of faith through the power of the spoken word.

January: Heart Check

My health may fail, and my spirit
may grow weak, but God remains the strength
of my heart; he is mine forever.
Psalm 73:26, NLT

In the last decade, have you let yourself go? Heart disease is the leading cause of death in women over forty. As you age, your heart muscle also ages and pumps less oxygen through your heart to your body. It takes more physical effort to increase your heart rate and longer to return to normal. God wants to help you address poor eating habits, lack of exercise, stress, and other issues affecting your heart's efficiency.

Thank You, God, for being the strength of my heart. As this year begins, cause me to love my heart as much as You do. You designed me to enjoy Your creation in nature and the foods I eat. Help me to be mindful of the body You've given me. Put Your desires in me, and cause my heart and spirit to align with Your best.

Today I will strengthen my heart through healthy
choices and time with the Lord.

Walk with Me

Come with me by yourselves
to a quiet place and get some rest.
Mark 6:31, NIV

On average, a person walks 3,000–4,000 steps a day. To be considered active, a person must walk more than 10,000 steps a day. Begin to monitor your daily steps for a week. Awareness increases diligence, and the rewards are great. Jesus would love to take a walk with you today. One of the most gratifying results of a daily walk with the Lord is appreciating His presence, clearing your mind, and then waiting upon Him in stillness.

Lord, as I begin my day, make me mindful of You. Help me carve some time out for a walk with You. Speak to me about what's on Your heart today. Hear my thoughts and prayers for myself and others. As I walk with You today, lead me to that quiet place where my problems lay at Your feet and I find Your rest.

Today I will walk in Your light, hear
Your voice, and find rest.

Healthy Bones

Prophesy to these bones and say to them,
"Dry bones, hear the word of the LORD!"
Ezekiel 37:4, NIV

We know the importance of calcium and vitamin D for healthy bones, especially for women over forty. Eating the right foods, getting the proper nutrients, and maintaining strength and weight-bearing help deter bone loss. Take some time to evaluate what your body needs, and make necessary adjustments. Added to your natural care is the power of Holy Spirit working in you every day. Begin to bless the areas of your body that need new life.

I thank You, Lord, for the wisdom and power of Your words to alert, protect, guide, and revive me. I ask for Your help to make healthy choices today. Speak to my spirit, and let that revelation through Your voice and Your Scriptures bring health to my body and strength to my bones.

**Today my whole body will thrive in the light of
God's Word as I speak life to my bones.**

His Peace

Lord, all my desire is before You;
And my sighing is not hidden from You.
Psalm 38:9, NKJV

Anything that lasts more than three months is considered chronic. It could be pain, insomnia, anxiety, migraines, or many other conditions. Sudden onsets are a shock, but the day-after-day trauma can make you weary. Your ability to cope challenges you and regular activity comes to a complete stop under the weight of long-term physical or mental demands. How are you handling chronic issues? The Lord wants to help you learn more and give you a fresh revelation to recapture His peace.

Lord, I have been frustrated with this constant challenge. I'm at the end of my rope. Hear my cry for help. I know I can change my attitude and take action, but other issues are beyond my control. Show me the root, give me direction and a way out of its grip, and lead me to Your peace. Open my ears to hear Your answer. Prince of Peace, come!

Today the Lord's ears are open to my cries,
and I will have peace with His answer.

Make Me Aware

Search me, O God, and know my heart;
test me and know my anxious thoughts.
Psalm 139:23, NLT

We are often unaware of subtle changes in our thinking. As the years go by, we don't perceive indirect influence on our mindsets. In many ways, we *go with the flow*. But is it a good flow, or are you affected by the world around you? The influence of society, culture, media, and technological advances shift your reasoning to their comfortable norms. Today is a good day to revisit your thinking.

Search my heart, Lord. I give You permission to bring past desires into greater focus. Have I left my dreams on a closet shelf or buried them in a forgotten journal? Show me where I have walked away from the destiny You prepared. Remind me of what once was and what can be. Spirit of truth, expose the lies I have believed and lead me to Your truth.

Today I will open my heart and mind to hear the Lord's thoughts about me.

Opportunities

JANUARY 6

Make the most of every opportunity.
Colossians 4:5, NLT

You turn the calendar on January 1st, and like most, want to turn a page on a troubling area of your life. Regrets can stay with you like swirling thoughts that never resolve. You can wallow in memories or decide it's time to take them to the Lord. Introspection and thoughtful consideration of an issue have a way of highlighting the source of the problem and even new pathways to freedom. The Good Shepherd of your soul goes before you and will lead you through the door of opportunity. Make the most of it.

Lord, I give You my concerns and troubled mind. I know You hear my every thought and prayer. Show me the adjustments I can make on my own. Give me Your peace for the areas I can't change and patience when I need to wait. Transform these challenges into opportunities to glorify Your name. You are my Good Shepherd. Lead me with Your voice.

**Today I will leave my regrets behind and
walk into new opportunities.**

Priority One

JANUARY 7

Seek the Kingdom of God above all else,
and live righteously, and he will
give you everything you need.
Matthew 6:33, NLT

Who takes precedence in your life? As you crawl out of bed, your thoughts turn to morning rituals of coffee, breakfast, and the day's priorities. This year, rethink and reprioritize your day. Setting the alarm fifteen minutes earlier could transform everything. A quiet breakfast with the King and His Word will greatly reward your soul and spirit. Peace comes when you are in His presence, and energy flows from that encounter.

Reorder my day, Lord. I choose to put You first. I delight in Your presence. Tell me Your dreams, and I'll tell You mine. Open my ears to hear Your voice. As I read Your Word, teach me Your will and ways. Open my mind to greater understanding. Give me wisdom, and show me how to navigate my day. May Your kingdom come and Your will be done this day.

Today the Lord will supply all I need
when I prioritize Him.

Weary No More

JANUARY 8

He gives strength to the weary
and increases the power of the weak.
Isaiah 40:29, NIV

Responsibilities have a way of draining your energy. Running to and fro to meet the needs of others depletes your physical and emotional reserves. This weariness means it's time to take stock of your burdens. The enemy of your peace comes to steal, kill, and destroy. Jesus comes with abundant life,[1] and Holy Spirit provides direction and guidance to show you a better way.

Lord, as this new year begins, show me the areas where I've taken too much responsibility. Help me find the source of my weariness and make adjustments. Give me a positive attitude of hope and expectation. Pour Your strength into my weak areas, and show me a better way. Encourage me, Holy Spirit, with Your wisdom. I will rejoice in You and Your gifts operating in me.

Today You will reveal what is mine
and what is Yours to manage.

Remember My Tears

JANUARY 9

You've kept track of all my wandering and my weeping.
You've stored my many tears in your bottle—not one will be lost.
For they are all recorded in your book of remembrance.
Psalm 56:8, TPT

Tears bring healing, whether from physical pain or heart wounds. They express deep emotion over pain, suffering, loss, and tragedy. His Word tells you to be brave, courageous, and strong. Learn from David, who wrote this psalm after he ran away from Saul. Appeal to the Father, who sees every one of your tears. They are precious to Him. Tears create endorphins, a natural painkiller that can produce positive feelings. A good cry is always healthy.

See my tears, Father, and my broken heart. Remember Your promise never to forsake or leave me, even when I feel abandoned and hopeless. See my tears, Father, for those I love who are suffering. Remember them in their times of need. Wipe away my tears, and remember Your promises.

Today I call upon the Lord to remember
my tears and answer my prayers.

Brighter Days Ahead

JANUARY 10

The path of the righteous is like the morning sun,
shining ever brighter till the full light of day.
Proverbs 4:18, NIV

Gray skies and gloomy winter days sometimes put us under the weather. We are familiar with many who seem to live in the glum 24/7. No matter what you say, they don't hear your encouragement. If you're honest, you can sometimes be in that same kind of funk. These are the times when worship takes you out of the storm and restores balance. When you give glory to the one who is the light, darkness has to flee!

Lord, You are my bright morning star. I praise Your matchless beauty. Your presence dispels darkness and gloom. Walk with me today. Go before me. Stand beside me. Guard my back. Keep me focused on You. Be my encouragement today. I will rejoice, walk free of doubt and unbelief, and enjoy Your light.

Today I will walk in the light of the Lord,
and darkness will flee.

Patient While Waiting

Wait for and *confidently expect the LORD;*
Be strong and let your heart take courage;
Yes, wait for and *confidently expect the LORD.*
Psalm 27:14, AMP

Every daughter feels the Lord has called her to do something special. Some are called to ministry, others to employment, and still others to the stability of their homes. That divine impartation keeps you pressing into His perfect plan for your life. Over years of unanswered prayers or delays, your spark might grow dimmer. This year, rekindle that dream and press through to your destiny.

Father, I trust that You hear my every prayer. I am Your well-loved child, and You are my loving Father. I have placed my petitions before Your throne for myself and others. Grant me peace and staying power to stand and keep standing until all of Your promises come true. May Your dreams and mine be fulfilled in my life.

**Today I will be fervent in my prayers and
wait patiently for His answer.**

Blind Spots

I will instruct you and teach you in
the way you should go;
I will guide you with My eye.
Psalm 32:8, NKJV

External situations or tunnel vision can impede our abilities to see what's right in front of us. As you aim to fulfill your resolutions, it's helpful to finetune and adjust your scope to bring clarity. False perceptions, outright lies, or wrong assumptions twist and entangle you. Ask the Lord to highlight what is true in your life and guide you with His vision.

Lord, remove the blinders from my eyes and help me see clearly. Forgive the limitations I have placed on myself. Show me the broad and narrow ways You have prepared for me. I open my heart, eyes, and ears to Your wisdom and revelation. Holy Spirit, expose the hidden barriers to my fruitfulness. Reveal the real me. I yield to Your perspective and ask for clear vision.

Today I will see as the Lord sees, and this revelation will free me from blind spots.

No Regrets

He lifted me out of the pit of despair,
out of the mud and the mire.
He set my feet on solid ground
and steadied me as I walked along.
Psalm 40:2, NLT

Deep disappointment or unfulfilled longings locks us up in despair. Endless battles and runarounds foil our efforts to get free. There is a way out of that pit. Let go of the past, and reach for Jesus's extended hand. Forgiving yourself is just as important as forgiving others. Regrets will keep you going around the mountain or stuck in a bottomless pit. This year, focus on the answer (Jesus) instead of your problems.

Jesus, You know what troubles me. You know my challenges, hurts, and wounds. You know everything about me. Help me let go of what holds me back. Prince of Peace, give me Your solutions for areas I can't change. Thank You for Your grace that lifts my head as I reach for Your hand.

Today I will get unstuck when I hold
Your hand and You lead me on.

15

Responsible Ones

And as for you, brothers and sisters,
never tire of doing what is good.
2 Thessalonians 3:13, NIV

One of the most challenging tasks we women face are our attitudes toward the responsibilities put upon us by ourselves, our families, and extended families. Aging parents face health and mental challenges. Children struggle with careers, finances, and childcare. You're caught in the middle, going out of your way to be helpful to both generations. In times like these, you need to take a second look at what's on your plate and move some over to God.

Lord, You know how much I want to help my loved ones. I am grateful for my health and willingness to do what I can when I can. When I pull away today to seek You and Your wisdom, show me what is necessary and what I need to let go. Take my worries and bring me Your peace. Help me to recognize the burdens I am fit to carry.

Today I give You my cares as You show me what to carry and what belongs to You.

Harmony

JANUARY 15

Behold, how good and how pleasant it is
For brothers to live together in unity!
Psalm 133:1, NASB

It takes two to harmonize and even more to create a symphony. Kitchens, backyards, workplaces, and even churches should have one thing in common—an atmosphere of acceptance and love. Women tend to be peacemakers, joy-bringers, and resolvers. You can sense when there is disquiet and instinctively work to *fix* the situation. There is no more excellent fixer than taking it to the Lord in prayer.

This year, Lord, help me to bring harmony into my home. Partner with me in this endeavor. Show me where I can cooperate with Your Spirit of love. Highlight the areas where my silent prayers will be most effective. Help me to be Your agent of goodwill whenever I interact with the world around me. Write Your harmony on my heart today, and may my song bring You glory.

Today I will be an instrument
of the Lord's peace wherever I go.

I Surrender My Time

Surrender your anxiety.
Be still and realize that I am God.
I am God above all the nations,
and I am exalted throughout the whole earth.
Psalm 46:10, TPT

Stillness is difficult when chaos rules. The Lord commands us to be still even in the midst of disorder and anxiety. Why is that? Perhaps it's for the Spirit of wisdom to have an opportunity to interject an answer, a plan, a new order, or a way out. When you pull away from the cares of the day and seek a quiet moment with Him, peace has a space to fill the void and centers you in His will.

Lord, I choose to put You first in my schedule. My calendar is in Your hands. You see my to-dos as well as my desires. As I pull away to worship You and read Your Word, show me Your priorities. Be the first and last of my day this year. I place all my worries in Your hands.

Today I will be free from anxiety when I surrender
my time and worries to the Lord.

Fresh Flow

He who believes in Me, as the Scripture has said,
out of his heart will flow rivers of living water.
John 7:38, NKJV

As days melt into weeks, we can lose sight of opportunities for redirection. We get trapped in the dreariness of daily tasks. One more trip to the grocery store, another sheet-changing day, and monthly bills to write can rob you of your joy. Winter woes inhabit your routines and relationships. Attitude is everything. Redirect your gaze, and step into His flow. Uncap your well, and let faith rise up to meet His promises.

Good Shepherd, lead me into Your fields of promise today. I feel buried in the mundane. I want to hear Your voice calling me to the hills. Open the gate of my heart. As I read Your Word, activate the river of life in me. Let my heart rejoice in Your fresh touch. Flow in and through me. Lighten these tasks with Your presence.

**Today I will read Your Word, and it will
release joy and refreshment.**

No Comparisons

Your hands have made me and established me;
Give me understanding and a teachable heart.
Psalm 119:73, AMP

When you measure yourself against others, you open up to self-criticism, disappointment, and even jealousy. Although comparing yourself can motivate you to make changes, it can also invite negative feelings of disqualification. We admire the gifted but criticize our shortcomings. Begin your day with confidence. You are who you are. The Lord can make you even better.

Lord, I long to be a better person. Jesus always said and did what His Father said and did. I also want to say and do the right thing at the right time. Give me revelation and understanding of what You've designed in and for me. Remove these negative thoughts and any barriers to the true me. Help me to use the unique gifts You deposited in me for Your glory.

Today I am uniquely gifted in the image of God
to shine, especially for Him.

Esteem One Another

Let *nothing* be done *through selfish ambition
or conceit, but in lowliness of mind
let each esteem others better than himself.*
Philippians 2:3, NKJV

"Esteem" is a well-earned recognition of truth, character, and the value or worth of a person. In today's culture, we often hear the terms self-esteem and self-respect. As you assess your nature this month, look deeply at your relationships. Who do you place highest on the pedestal of your heart? Yourself? Your spouse? Your children? Who has the preeminence? You may need to adjust who receives the most attention.

Lord, I humble myself before You. You are first and foremost in my heart. Thank You for the gifts and talents You've given to me. I want to use them for Your glory as I interact with those around me. When pride rears its head, gently tug on my heart. Show me how I can affirm my family, friends, and coworkers even before myself.

**Today I will look for ways to esteem
the Lord and others.**

The Price of Pearls

JANUARY 20

When he discovered a pearl of great value,
he sold everything he owned and bought it!
Matthew 13:46, NLT

Unresolved issues scream, "No way out, around, over, or through." Consider a single piece of sand in an oyster. All that irritation can take from six months to four years to produce a pearl. In the end, the process was necessary for such a great reward. Unanswered challenges with your family or coworkers can rob you of peace and joy. What issues can you resolve, and what should you leave with Him?

Lord, You know everything that's on my heart. You see the end from the beginning. But, Lord, I am weary of trying to do this alone. Give me clarity and direction for changes I can make. Give me Your peace for things only You can change. Strengthen my resolve and transform my attitude. Produce Your pearl in me.

Today I will have peace as You produce
a pearl of great beauty in me.

Delays

For since the world began, no ear has
heard and no eye has seen a God like you,
who works for those who wait for him!
Isaiah 64:4, NLT

With patient endurance, we persevere in faith. One day passes into another, but hope deferred is not in your vocabulary. You persist. You pursue. You push through. How is that possible? Only with an unshakeable faith can you bravely ride the storms of life through to victory. The timing of your promises is up to God, but He's given His word to you.

Long ago, You spoke words of promise into my heart. They were promises for me and my loved ones. Help me to revisit them. Rekindle the fire in my heart for those promises. You know my every need. I trust You to complete what You have started. Even in these delays, I will trust You. You will always have my best interest at heart. I will wait with expectancy.

Today I will wait calmly and praise You
as my Father, who knows best.

Burdens: Mine or Yours?

*Cast your burden upon the LORD
and He will sustain you.*
Psalm 55:22, NASB

Women are fixers. Instinctively, we bandage wounds, dry tears, and run to the rescue time and time again. There are only so many hours in the day. If you overbook yourself with everyone else's needs, there's little time left over for your needs. As you look at what's on your plate this year, revisit your have-tos and should-dos with His must-dos. The Lord delights in sharing your burdens. But then, He needs your *me* time too.

Lord, You designed me to be a responsible, caring person. I'm good at what I do, and I thank You for those gifts. Sometimes, I just get overwhelmed with this heavy load. Help me to recognize when I take on too much. Give me insight into what is my responsibility and what belongs to others. Teach me how to cast my burdens onto Your strong shoulders.

**Today I will cast my burdens onto the Lord
and anticipate His victory.**

Early Rising

JANUARY 23

*I love those who love me; And those who seek me
early* and *diligently will find me.*
Proverbs 8:17, AMP

Mornings can be hectic or ordered by choice. You must spend precious time with the one who created you to rediscover who you are. That takes commitment. If you want to change, you need intentional moments with the keeper of your soul (mind, will, and emotions). You will find your reward in His delight. His Word never fails. The root word for the phrase "those who seek me diligently" is only one word: dawn.[1] Mornings matter to the Lord.

Lord, I want to draw nearer to You each day. As I set my alarm to awaken early, meet me in my quiet place. I long to know You better. Let me hear Your counsel as I commune with You and read Your Word. Speak to me between the lines. Show me Your heart and mine. Set the rhythm of my day as I begin it with You.

**Today Your presence will remain
throughout my day.**

Stillness

*He calmed the storm to a whisper
and stilled the waves.*
Psalm 107:29, NLT

Complex family relationships, unreconciled problems, quarrels, and complaints can wear you down. Stormy situations can drain your energy, tax your emotions, and disturb your sleep. Everything in you yells, "Quiet!" Problem-solvers, women who work hard to bring peace at any price, sometimes need to withdraw to a quiet place with the Lord. When you cultivate friendship with the Lord, you activate His dominion over your challenges. In the stillness, you will hear His answer.

Father, today I have a laundry list of problems to lay at Your feet. I am so grateful for this quiet time with you. As I still my thoughts and open my heart to hear Your voice, speak to me. I need Your wisdom to look long and hard at these unresolved issues. Show me Your priorities, and give me Your strategies for the days ahead.

**Today peace will reign when the Lord
speaks to the storms around me.**

Am I Thirsty?

JANUARY 25

I thirst for you, my whole being longs for you,
in a dry and parched land where there is no water.
Psalm 63:1, NIV

Health experts recommend that women drink at least eleven or more cups of water daily to lubricate joints, regulate body temperature, and rid the body of waste. You are a triune being with a body, a soul, and a spirit. The cares of the world can drain your resources in all three areas. Jesus gave the antidote to the Samaritan woman.[1] The water He provides is the living water that becomes a fresh, bubbling spring of eternal life.

Lord, there's a deep longing inside for something more. Days keep drifting on without a refreshing touch from You. As I commit to drawing near to You daily, satisfy this thirst in me. Uncap my well, and release the flow of Your Spirit. Help me to drink deeply from Your river of life.

Today I will satisfy my thirst in Your presence
when we draw each other near.

Up, Periscope

JANUARY 26

I pray that your hearts will be flooded with light
so that you can understand the confident hope he has
given to those he called—his holy people
who are his rich and glorious inheritance.
Ephesians 1:18, NLT

A periscope operates by light striking a mirror and then reflecting the image for viewing. That's what the Word of God does for you. Jesus is the light of the world. As you read His Word, His light, through Holy Spirit's revelation, reflects His truth on the mirror of your heart. It transforms your thinking, motivates your actions, and radiates His light in your world—all for His glory.

Fill me, Lord, with Your light. As I read Your Word, open the eyes
of my heart to see You more clearly. I won't withdraw from Your
light. I am determined to grow and mature. Reveal the shadows in
my heart. Gently touch my nature, and make me more like You. I
long to reflect Your beauty and majesty to those around me.

Today I open my heart for the Lord's light
to shine through me.

Guide Me

But when he, the Spirit of truth, comes,
he will guide you into all the truth.
John 16:13, NIV

As believers, one of the greatest gifts we receive with salvation is our companion, Holy Spirit. He is ever-present within you and delights in showing you the way of righteousness. As you grow in Him, His fruit matures as your character becomes more like Jesus. His wisdom pricks your conscience, leads you on the right path, and convicts you when you miss the mark.

Holy Spirit, help me to understand Your ways better. I want to know You fully this year. Open the Scriptures and give me revelation to understand the deeper things of God. Take me on a journey with You. Be my companion and teacher. Show me where I've headed down the wrong path, and guide me into a walk that reflects the character of Jesus. May Your fruit and gifts grow into maturity this year.

Today I will receive an increase from Holy Spirit
after He guides me into all truth.

Rabbit Trails

JANUARY 28

Then we will no longer be immature like children.
We won't be tossed and blown about by every wind of new teaching.
We will not be influenced when people try to trick us with
lies so clever they sound like the truth.
Ephesians 4:14, NLT

Rabbit ears twitch this way and that, depending on the direction of the sound. They hop with boundless energy, this way and that, as curiosity calls. You, too, can get caught up with various media. As this month of reflection and assessment draws to a close, ask Holy Spirit what to keep and what to reject. Let Him guide the new you to the *me* He created you to be.

Lord, opportunities abound with social media, podcasts, books, newsletters, and conferences. I want to learn more about You, Your kingdom, and my role in it. Give me discernment for the best use of my time. I don't want to have itching ears for the latest and greatest. I just want Your best for me.

Today I will listen carefully as
Holy Spirit guides me.

Overflowing

Give, and it will be given to you.
A good measure, pressed down, shaken together
and running over, will be poured into your lap.
For with the measure you use, it will be measured to you.
Luke 6:38, NASB

The law of sowing and reaping is permanently fixed in our minds, whether from reading the Old or New Testament. Sowing refers to planting, and reaping refers to harvesting. You will harvest whatever seeds you sow into your relationship with the Lord. Those seeds could be time, prayer, finances, or acts of kindness. As you close this month of reflection on where you are and where you want to be, ask the Lord what's on His list.

Father, thank You for all You've done for me this past year. As I set
my goals for the year ahead, show me where You want me to grow
the most. I want to see You increase in my life. May I overflow to
others from Your bounty.

Today I will ask the Lord for new
seeds to sow this year.

Required of Me

He has shown you, O man, what is good;
And what does the LORD require of you,
but to do justly, to love mercy,
and to walk humbly with your God?
Micah 6:8, NKJV

More than anything, we desire our lives to be true and righteous and bring honor to God. That's not always easy when we deal with life's hiccups—those unforeseen situations where we have to drop everything to meet an emergency. The Father knows your limitations. He also knows what you are capable of. Today's verse underscores three godly virtues: justice, mercy, and humility.

Give me grace, Lord, to love others as You do. Jesus, as the judge
of my life, teach me patience and fairness. Help me to be balanced.
As the lover of my soul, help me be merciful and kind to others. As
the model for my spirit, Holy Spirit, increase Your fruit in my life.
Train me to serve with a humble heart.

Today I submit to Your leading in justice,
mercy, and humility.

Renewed Vision

JANUARY 31

Create in me a clean heart, O God;
and renew a right spirit within me.
Psalm 51:10, KJV

We've looked at ourselves from different angles this month. God is creating fresh enthusiasm for what has become ho-hum in your life. He desires to remove the stale and moldy and brush away the cobwebs so that your spirit, soul, and body find rejuvenation this year. Can't you sense the fire and wind of Holy Spirit renewal?

Thank You, Father, for what You've done for me this past month. My faith declarations lift my heart and confidence. They are the new foundation bricks You are rebuilding in me. Jesus, the Word of God, is my cornerstone. Holy Spirit, continue to clean my heart. Monitor my motives. Nudge me back onto Your path when I stray. Keep me pure in all my ways. I will accomplish all You've put on my heart for this year.

Today I thank You, Lord, for loving me as I am
and helping me fulfill Your dream.

February

DO I KNOW WHO I REALLY AM?

Now that we've spent the first month looking honestly at ourselves and where we want to be by the year's end, let's change our perspectives to discover *who* we are relative to our roles. We begin with our creator. You were formed in His image to display His glory. Once you embrace your uniqueness, you will affect others with His special light and love placed just in you.

As women, we tend to define ourselves by our looks, accomplishments, careers, and even families. This month, the Scriptures, food for thought, prayers, and declarations will focus on your relationships in an ever-widening circle of influence, beginning as a unique child of God. The weeks that follow will highlight relationships as a woman, daughter, sister, spouse/single, and finally, spiritual sister to the church and your peers.

Skillfully Made

You even formed every bone in my body
when you created me in the secret place;
carefully, skillfully you shaped me
from nothing to something.
Psalm 139:15, TPT

There is no one like *you* in the world. The master craftsman designed you so uniquely that no two are alike. You not only look different, but you also differ in temperament, intelligence, and personality. These factors don't even include the place and time of your birth or the socioeconomic and cultural effects on the *me* you've become. Even with all these possibilities, God created you to be exceptional and wonderful in His eyes.

Thank You, Father, for shaping my body in the secret place of just You and me. No one knows me like You do. You designed me to be this tall, with this hair and these features. May the woman I am on the inside reflect the carefully and skillfully shaped body You made for me on the outside.

Today I declare I am God's masterpiece
and a trophy for His shelf.

Born for Now

And who knows whether you have
attained royalty for such a time as this
[and for this very purpose]?
Esther 4:14, AMP

Although God knows the end from the beginning, His purpose for your life is still dependent on your choices. To ensure you fulfill that purpose, He's gifted you with stretchability. We live in a historical era in which technology doubles every two years. It boggles the mind. And yet, the Father knew who He needed on this earth and at this time. He anointed you to ride that wave with determination and skill.

Lord, I have seen so much change these many years. The quiet, unrushed days of youth are gone, and the pull and pace of my days are sometimes beyond my comprehension. It's so hard to keep up. You have a plan for me. You placed me right here, right now, and for the right reason. Give me the wisdom I need for these fast-paced times.

Today I am Your handmaiden and will fulfill
Your purpose for my day.

Under Your Shadow

Because you are my help,
I sing in the shadow of your wings.
I cling to you; your right hand upholds me.
Psalm 63:7–8, NIV

Age doesn't matter to your Father. You are still His child. You will always be His child. You might think you will have it all together once you reach forty. Not so. There is a child in you who will always need protection, comfort, direction, and affirmation. When there's no one and nowhere else to turn, you can still run to the Father, take His hand, and envelop yourself in His loving arms.

Abba, You are still my Daddy. Thank You for leading me by Your hand through these decades. You've been with me through every phase. You uphold me even when doubts about myself take me to a dark place. Thank You for being the light that shows me the way to Your embrace. You soothe the little girl in me and strengthen the woman of grace I am becoming.

Today I will take the Father's hand into
His secret place above the storms.

Priceless

And even the very hairs of your head are all numbered.
Matthew 10:30, NIV

The Father knows best, and the Father knows all. Abba reassures us that nothing escapes His view. He sees your trials, tests, and temptations. He has seen what you've faced and the scars that remain. How do you know this? Jesus, a human being just like you, faced trials, tests, and temptations too. The Father didn't abandon Jesus until it was time for our Savior to take our place and our sins. Take heart! The Father won't ever abandon you.

My spirit rejoices in You, Father. You know everything about me. You number the hairs on my head and even those in my brush. Such awareness is incomprehensible to me. You observe every challenge in my life. You dry my tears and encourage my heart. My skinned knees may be a thing of the past, but today, I want to skip into Your embrace. Daddy, can I have a hug?

**Today I will bless the Lord, for His
loving arms hold me close.**

Rod and Staff

Yea, though I walk through the valley of the shadow of death,
I will fear no evil; For You are with me;
Your rod and Your staff, they comfort me.
Psalm 23:4, NKJV

When we plant a new tree, we secure the sapling to stakes with flexible bands. These stakes stabilize the tree against heavy winds, and the bands allow the trunk to bend but not break. Movement is vital so roots can grow deep and strong. As the tree matures, the stakes move farther away until removed altogether. Like David, the Lord's rod of correction and staff of direction comfort you as you walk through the shadows to His light.

Lord, correction is never easy. I recognize its worth in building a better me, but some things from my earlier years have left deep wounds. As a mature woman, I still wince when I receive a rebuke. Heal the wounds of the past so I can receive correction with Your grace.

Today I will be set free from childhood pain
and cling to Your rod and staff.

Trained by Love

FEBRUARY 6

For the Lord's training of your life is the evidence
of his faithful love. And when he draws you to himself,
it proves you are his delightful child.
Hebrews 12:6, TPT

There is nothing quite like getting pricked in your conscience when you say or do something you know isn't right. There's an "uh-oh" alarm bell that goes off inside. We immediately want to take it back, grab it out of the air, or trash that text or email. Now and then, our sainthood slips. When this happens, honesty is always the best policy—especially with the Lord, who *is* love.

Lord, this fleshly me struggles. Sometimes, I let the old me slip out, which upsets me. I want to be grown up, mature, and pleasing in all my ways. Holy Spirit, keep nudging me the way You do. I appreciate the checks and delight in Your corrections. They never hurt. They set me free to love myself and others.

Today I will delight in Your loving correction.

Go to Him

FEBRUARY 7

*Let all the little children come to me
and never hinder them! Don't you know
that God's kingdom exists for such as these?*
Mark 10:14, TPT

It doesn't matter what age we are. We are still children to the Father, sisters to Jesus, and students of Holy Spirit. The Lord sees your struggles as well as your triumphs. He longs for you to take everything to Him. You may be mature, but you still need a daddy, a big brother, and a best friend. You are never too old to cry. You are never too old to be held.

Abba, I'm still your little girl. I look up to You and trust Your love. I'm not too old that you can't correct me. My heart is always open to You, Your correction, and Your direction. You've dried my tears, removed my shame, and set me on Your kingdom's path. Thank You for Your open arms and loving embrace.

**Today I will go to Him with all my hidden fears,
and He will hear me.**

Laughing with Joy

FEBRUARY 8

She is clothed with strength and dignity,
and she laughs without fear of the future.
Proverbs 31:25, NLT

You can never hold back time, but you can relish the growth it brings. As women mature, our manner develops a certain regal grace. You learn from your girlhood mistakes and make adjustments thanks to Holy Spirit's guidance into womanhood. The wisdom and intuitive nature He builds in you become the backbone of any family or organization.

Lord, thank You for designing me to be a woman. I don't feel like the weaker sex. I feel confident and capable because of You and what You've taught me through these years. You've strengthened my inner life. You've walked me through some tough times. You've been my ever-present companion. Your Word has held me together. It's given me focus, encouragement, and direction. Receive my praise and thanksgiving. I want to bring You glory.

Today I will laugh and rejoice for what my future holds.

Trusted with More

*We do, however, speak a message of wisdom among the
mature, but not the wisdom of this age or of the rulers of this
age, who are coming to nothing.*
1 Corinthians 2:6, NIV

The saying goes that we women have eyes in the back of our heads. That's probably a very true statement. A woman's intuition seems woven into the Father's design. He has deposited a Holy Ghost radar in you that picks up on the atmosphere and subtle changes in your surroundings. You sense when things just aren't right. With maturity, you rise to the battle and speak with boldness.

Lord, this sensitivity to light and darkness, and right and wrong, is Your gift. Thank You for this skill. Rather than being broadsided with situations, You help me anticipate the steps I need to take to thwart the enemy's moves. You've given me Your Word that instructs me and Your Spirit that directs me. Increase this gift of discernment. I choose to operate in all You've given me.

**Today I will be alert to the enemy's hidden plans
and have the Lord's answers.**

Refined by Fire

FEBRUARY 10

This third I will put into the fire; I will refine them
like silver and test them like gold. They will call on my
name and I will answer them; I will say, "They are my
people," and they will say, "The LORD is our God."
Zechariah 13:9, NIV

At midlife, we look back at the many fires we've passed through. Careers, marriage, relocation, illness, and financial woes are only a partial list of what most of us face. Some of us thrive on confrontation. Others are more delicate. But you know this: you belong to the Lord, and He will bring you through.

Oh Lord, I probably smell like smoke from the fires I've been through over the years. It hasn't been easy. Thank You for being faithful and never giving up on me. I sometimes wonder why so many issues were on my shoulders. But then, I recognize that You've always been there to show me the way through the fire.

Today, Lord, refine me in Your fire.

Daughter

"Daughter," he said to her,
"your faith has made you well. Go in peace."
Luke 8:48, NLT

Do you remember when you first felt the Lord's touch or heard His voice? Unforgettable. Everything within you shook with excitement and wonderment. The God of the universe sees and hears you! One of Jesus's most memorable miracles is healing the woman with the twelve-year issue of blood. Jesus called her daughter. He recognized her pain, her need, and her faith. We may experience delays, but the answer is always near.

Oh Jesus, I love how You called that poor woman daughter. You were on Your way somewhere else, but You felt her touch. It moved You so much that You stopped to search for her. Lord, would You touch my need today? I long to feel Your nearness and hear Your voice. I need healing too. Some things have long been on my heart. Hear me and heal me now.

Today I will hear Your voice and feel Your touch.

Martha, Martha

"Martha, Martha," the Lord answered,
"you are worried and upset about many things,
but few things are needed—or indeed only one.
Mary has chosen what is better, and it will
not be taken away from her."
Luke 10:41–42, NIV

Imagine you're Martha, and you've got a house full of people, a meal to serve, and Jesus, *the* rabbi, is the guest of honor. Martha is flustered and needs help. We can all say, "Been there. Done that." You wish you could be like Mary, sitting at His feet, but then you have work to do! Don't lose sight of Jesus calling her name twice—that's a form of endearment. As you mature, you learn what's essential and what can wait.

After all these years, I just have to thank You, Lord, for giving me the grace to wait and be patient. Grocery stores, banks, and checkout counters have become opportunities to smile, visit, and encourage others. To be honest, I could use a bit more grace today.

Today I will spend the good part of my day
with You, Jesus, and pass it on.

Resplendent

God, you are so resplendent and radiant! Your
majesty shines from your everlasting mountain.
Nothing could be compared to you in glory!
Psalm 76:4, TPT

Have you ever thought of yourself as resplendent? You are! As women, we are created in God's image from His glory to reflect His glory. "Resplendent" in Hebrew means to be or become light. Just as His light shines radiantly, His light in you can shine out to a dark world.[1] There is majesty and grace in your femininity that only womanhood can express. Like the Father, you are supple, graceful, nurturing, and tender.

I can't imagine what it would be like to see You, Lord, in all Your
glory. I think of Moses, Isaiah, Ezekiel, Peter, John, and James on
the Mount of Transfiguration. It fills me with such expectation for
that day. Open my eyes today, and give me a peek at Your splendor.
And then, Lord, show me how I reflect You.

Today I will see myself through the Father's eyes.

Be My Valentine

FEBRUARY 14

I pray that your love will overflow more and more,
and that you will keep on growing
in knowledge and understanding.
Philippians 1:9, NLT

The more time you spend reading the Word of God, the more you realize how loved you are. Holy Spirit constantly woos you into a deeper relationship. He writes His affection and desires into your heart with every word and every story. His Word is a love letter. Holy Spirit unlocks revelation and a greater understanding of that love every time you read Scripture. Today, of all days, send a love letter to Jesus through your prayers.

My heart just overflows with gratitude, well, for everything. Father, You designed me out of love to know love. Jesus, You first loved me and gave Your life for me. Holy Spirit, You drew me to Jesus and opened my heart to receive forgiveness and learn to walk in Your light. Lord, will You be my valentine today and every day?

Today I will sing a song of love to the Lord.

Bride-to-Be

FEBRUARY 15

Your presence releases a fragrance so pleasing—over
and over poured out. For your lovely name is "Flowing Oil."
No wonder the brides-to-be adore you.
Song of Solomon 1:3, TPT

Falling in love is a once-in-a-lifetime experience. Everything within us reaches out to the man of our dreams. You yearn for his company. You listen for the phone to ring with an offer of a next date. Remember your first love when you were captivated by that unquenchable longing? The same is true when the Lord reveals Himself to your heart for the first time. His presence awakens love.

I remember falling in love. It was breathtaking, exciting, and even sometimes scary. I couldn't wait to see my beloved again. That's how I feel about You, Jesus. The day I said, "I do," was like the day I said, "I believe. Forgive me for my sins." Everything seemed alive and filled with promise. Jesus, You are my beloved forever. Keep that spark in my marriage and our relationship.

Today my heart will walk down the aisle
with You again, Jesus.

Power of Agreement

*Again, I give you an eternal truth: If two of you agree
to ask God for something in a symphony of prayer,
my heavenly Father will do it for you.*
Matthew 18:19, TPT

In the beginning, one of the most excellent partnerships the Father designed was husband and wife. When you leave your parents' home and authority, two individuals become one in His eyes. Inviting the Lord into your decisions brings the best conclusion. Why? God honors unity and shared responsibility. He doesn't want you to go it alone. He wants to be in the middle of it all.

Oh Father, sometimes I don't agree with my husband. As we bring our plans to You, I trust that You will protect me, my husband, and our children in our choices. I look to You to guide us through Your Word, our prayers, and the principles You've taught us. Hear our prayers and answer us. Lead us always to victory.

**Today the Lord will strengthen my marriage
through the power of agreement.**

Champion Friend

To the widow he is a champion friend.
The lonely he makes part of a family.
Psalm 68:5, TPT

In other translations, this verse describes the Lord as judge, defender, advocate, and protector. "Champion" is excellent, but I would add "lover" for the widow and "companion" for the lonely. Widowed and single women struggle with depression, finances, and discrimination, among other issues. But our God promises to care and watch over women such as these. Discarded and abandoned to make it on her own, Hagar is an example to us. She met El Roi, "The God Who Sees Me," and survived.[1]

Lord, thank You for Your watchful eye. You tenderly watch over this daughter and see to my needs. Even when I feel abandoned, You are the lover of my soul. You lift my spirits and show me a brighter way. You console my heart and bring others into my life for comfort and companionship. Help me to be an instrument of such love to others in need.

Today I will remember the widowed
and lonely as the Lord does.

Brokenhearted

FEBRUARY 18

He heals the brokenhearted And binds up their wounds.
Psalm 147:3, NKJV

We are inconsolable when we lose a dear one's life, a relationship, or even an opportunity. The chasm of hopelessness is so deep that, sometimes, you see no way out of the pit of despair. That's precisely the time for faith to arise and confession of His promises. God never lies. His promises are true. The Father made you strong, but He recognizes your need when all seems lost. He sees your tears, hears your cries, and He will answer.

Lord, I have lost count of the times I've sunk to my knees with grief. You have always met me in my pool of tears. I don't know where I get the strength to get up and go on, but I know it's You. I have felt Your arms around me, bringing peace to my heart. Thank You, Abba. I can always run to You and Your Word. Your promises strengthen me.

**Today I declare You are God who
heals the brokenhearted.**

Like-Minded

*Make my joy complete by being like-minded, having
the same love, being one in spirit and of one mind.*
Philippians 2:2, NIV

Sometimes, families just don't get along. You give some grace for
bad moods, but it's time for an intervention when disagreeable
behavior becomes a habit. This disruption of your peace and unity is
especially true in your home. Women are called the heart of the
home for a reason. When discord enters, the enemy follows and
takes up residence. That's why we arm ourselves with His Word,
which says we have the mind of Christ.[1]

*Lord, Your Word and ways establish love, peace, harmony, and
unity. Without You in my home, we are lost. Give me Your wisdom
to expose underlying issues. Show me strategies to root out the
enemy's influence on myself and my family. I open my heart to any
fault I might have. Expose my part, and give me the grace to
restore Your order to my home.*

**Today my family will be one in love,
spirit, and mind.**

United in Love

*My goal is that they may be encouraged in heart
and united in love, so that they may have the full
riches of complete understanding, in order that they
may know the mystery of God, namely, Christ.*
Colossians 2:2, NIV

Have you ever been at a family gathering where you felt incredible joy? Weddings and baby showers are like that. You sense complete harmony, unity, and love in times like these. There is a *oneness* that no outsider can break. Jesus's prayer was that all might be one with Him and the Father.[1]

Jesus, You chose to perform Your first miracle at a wedding. I love how Your mother went to You when they needed more wine. I remember Your parable about the ten virgins waiting for the Bridegroom. I think about the marriage feast in my future when we will be united forever. You're not so mysterious. You love weddings, and I love You.

**Today I will remember beautiful gatherings
and imagine Jesus there.**

True and Faithful

A wife of noble character is her husband's crown.
Proverbs 12:4, NIV

Relationships, especially marriage, have ups and downs over the years. These peaks and valleys are especially true as you become familiar with their quirks. Sometimes, you just laugh and shake your head, but other times, their behavior and words can be annoying, disappointing, and even hurtful. That's where grace pours in, and our covenant of love stands against the test. Like Jesus, you are true and faithful to the ones you love.

Lord Jesus, You've taught me the power of grace and forgiveness in relationships with Your disciples. They argued, jockeyed for position, and even abandoned You. In some ways, I'm just like them. But Jesus, You took pity on the hungry and helpless. You healed the wounded, diseased, and demon-possessed. Help me, Lord, to obey Your commandment to love one another as You have loved us.

**Today I will seek a new way to enrich
my relationships.**

Sisterhood

A man who has *friends must himself be friendly,*
But there is a friend who *sticks closer than a brother.*
Proverbs 18:24, NKJV

God has endowed women with a maternal and nurturing character. A well of compassion rises in us when we are with someone who is hurting. Our first instinct is to bring comfort. That quality comes straight from the heart of our Father. Deeper still, only trust and time allow you to open up your true self to your friends and remove the public mask you wear. Oddly enough, the friend who sticks closer than a sister already sees the mask and loves you, just like the Father does. It works both ways.

Thank You, Father, for the dear friends You've placed in my life. Some have moved away. Some are too busy with heavy responsibilities. Some are in difficult times and have isolated themselves from me. You've put their faces in front of my heart. I bring them to You, Father, one by one, in prayer.

Today I will listen for the Lord's
prompt for my friend's sake.

Supporting in Love

And out of your reverence for Christ
be supportive of each other in love.
Ephesians 5:21, TPT

As sisters-in-Christ, one of the best ways we can support one another is with our sensitivity. How often have you felt alone in a personal struggle? It might surprise you that we can read it in your face, see it in your posture, and hear it in your voice. The Shepherd of your soul knows it too. That's why He created His church to be the ones who help carry your burdens. We are His hands and feet. Let us carry you.

Jesus, I love Your Parable of the Lost Sheep where You left the ninety-nine for the one. Sometimes, I've felt like that one. I tend to want to do it myself, and sometimes I hide the real me, even from my friends. Thank You for loving me through them when they call me out of my funk. Show me who is hurting so I can give them a boost of love like You've given me.

Today I will find someone who needs a love tap.

As Unto the Lord

If I were doing this on my own initiative,
I would deserve payment. But I have no choice,
for God has given me this sacred trust.
1 Corinthians 9:17, NLT

Do you pay attention to those who provide for you and your family every Sunday at church? They are the faithful ones, serving consistently without complaint. There are greeters, ushers, prayer warriors, basket holders, teachers, aides, communion passers, worship singers and players, and the audio-visual crew. This list doesn't even include those out of sight. The Lord notices. These are the ones who will be first in His kingdom.

King Jesus, I want to bring these servants and handmaidens who serve in my church to Your throne room. No, Your church. Lord, bless them for their faithfulness to care for the needs of the body of Christ. They sacrifice their time and energy and serve with joy week after week. Bless their homes with Your presence and favor. Lord, I try to do my part, but if there is something more I can do, would You show me?

Today I will acknowledge those who serve You.

Our Song Matters

I will sing of the LORD's unfailing love forever!
Young and old will hear of your faithfulness.
Psalm 89:1, NLT

Young children model what they observe. Teenagers hide behind their shells. Young adults begin to test their independence. With maturity, we sing with grace and confidence. The Lord takes pleasure in our songs of love and gratitude. He especially delights when all the generations join together. When Pharaoh's chariots and horsemen were swallowed in the sea, Miriam sang, danced, and played her tambourine before the Lord. The women followed her.

My Lord and King Jesus, I may not have the best voice or the most graceful moves, but receive my song and praise for all You have done. Whether alone with You now or in public, I am not ashamed to shout, sing, and dance before You. Give me the boldness to express this joy to the younger generation. Use me to ignite a renewed passion for praise.

Today I will sing a new song to the Lord.

Living Out Loud

You are living letters written by Christ, not with ink
but by the Spirit of the living God—not carved onto stone
tablets but on the tablets of tender hearts.
2 Corinthians 3:3, TPT

The Lord entrusts you to demonstrate His goodness to the next generation. He's met you every step as you've matured in your spiritual journey. You have hard-won lessons to impart. Long hours with paper Bibles and research books yield a wealth of wisdom. Worldly knowledge has increased, but what of the younger generation's understanding of *Him* and His ways? You can be a joy-bringer and life-giver by living your faith out loud.

Holy Spirit, today's fast-paced world leaves little time for deeper study and more interaction with You and Your Word. My heart hurts for the younger generations and their challenges in our highly technical world. There are apps for everything, even Your Word. Give me opportunities to share the inspiration You've given me over the years. Create opportunities for me to encourage them. Help me to see their needs and meet them.

Today I will live my faith out loud
with someone younger than me.

Encouragement

FEBRUARY 27

Be of good courage, And He shall strengthen your heart,
All you who hope in the LORD.
Psalm 31:24, NKJV

Throughout the Old and New Testaments, Holy Spirit constantly reminds us to be bold and have good courage. Even in despair, when David and his men lost everything, David encouraged himself in the Lord and received a victorious answer.[1] The Lord has given you this great gift of encouragement for yourself and others. You know how to rally around one another with a word, personal support, and prayer. That's the beauty of sisterhood. It must surely please the Lord.

Lord, I want to thank You for my dear friends who encourage me when I am down and out. They strengthen my spirit in so many ways. I recognize that their goodness comes from their relationships with You. I ask You to bless them doubly today for the hope they've given me. And, Lord, show me someone I can encourage.

Today I will bless the Lord for His
goodness through my friends.

Overflowing Fullness

And from the overflow of his fullness we received
grace heaped upon more grace!
John 1:16, TPT

We match our calendars with solar years every four years by adding an extra day. It's like we get a bonus day to reap an added harvest. This verse follows John the Baptist's announcement that Jesus is *the one* we've all been waiting for. If you could only grasp the magnitude of the Father's plan, Jesus's willingness, and Holy Spirit's preparation! Let grace and more grace fill your heart today as you meditate on all that Jesus did for you. It just might make you want to leap!

Oh Jesus! My heart leaps with boundless joy and delight that You came into my life. I made You the King of my everything. Thank You for the extravagant grace You poured into me with Holy Spirit. I love His wisdom, counsel, and teaching! And all of this came to me because of Your sacrifice. All glory to You, my Lord.

Today I will dance and leap with joy.

March

WHO IS THE HIDDEN ME?

We've progressed from *where* we are to *who* we are with God and others. This month, we're going to do some soul-searching and spirit-listening. Israel was set free after 430 years in captivity. They experienced miracles in Goshen and left Egypt healed and wealthy. They saw the Red Sea part, Pharaoh's army defeated, water flowing out of a rock, and manna and quail falling from heaven. They even had the Lord's presence with the cloud by day and the pillar of fire by night.

When the people heard the thunder and the loud blast of the ram's horn, and when they saw the flashes of lightning and the smoke billowing from the mountain, they stood at a distance, trembling with fear. And they said to Moses, "You speak to us, and we will listen. But don't let God speak directly to us, or we will die!"
Exodus 20:18–19, NLT

Despite all these magnificent displays of the Father's love and power, they couldn't face their God. Why? Their bodies left captivity, but their souls and spirits did not. This month, we will flip the script on deception, past wounds, unforgiveness, false identity, bad habits, and cultural stereotypes with declarations that let us free.

My Hearing Ear

MARCH 1

Tune your ears to wisdom,
and concentrate on understanding.
Proverbs 2:2, NLT

We are bombarded with conflicting voices every day. TV channels, social media, phones, watches, and cars are all talking nonstop. There are even cloud-based AI voices known as Alexa and Siri that live in a box in our homes. Our generation has experienced a massive increase of noise from these voices. But whose voice should you be listening to? With all this competition, Holy Spirit has little opportunity to speak to you about what is on His heart.

Holy Spirit, forgive me for not stepping away from all the noise to seek quiet time with You. You have very little chance to get through to me as I flit from computer to TV, iPad, and various other sources. Help me to pull away and seek You. Join me in my quiet time and speak to me. Tune my ears to Your still, small voice. It's Your voice I want to hear. I need You. I need Your wisdom.

Today I will stop and listen
for Holy Spirit to speak.

My Seeing Eye

MARCH 2

The eye is the lamp of the body. If your eyes are healthy,
your whole body will be full of light.
Matthew 6:22, NIV

Our eyes collect light from our environments, transmit signals to our brains, and cause reactions. What you see affects how you move and how your heart feels. Spiritual eyes are similar. *What* or *who* do you have your eyes fixed on? You can be single-eyed in focus or dart from here to there. The Lord has created a world of beauty and your own eyes to capture and treasure it. Perhaps it's time to refocus.

Lord, forgive me when I've let my eyes see too much. Protect my
soul and spirit from allowing darkness to creep in. Cleanse me
from traumatic scenes in my life from childhood up to today. Bring
Your pure light into those situations. I take responsibility and
confess my part for what I have allowed my eyes to see. Heal me
now, in Jesus's name.

Today I will open my eyes to see Your beauty.

My Words

MARCH 3

A soft answer turns away wrath,
But a harsh word stirs up anger.
Proverbs 15:1, NKJV

Sometimes, we can be our worst enemy with our words about ourselves and others. Kind words heal, encourage, honor, and bless. Harsh words bite, hurt, offend, and curse. In the beginning, God created life with His spoken words. Additionally, in the beginning, the serpent created doubt with his spoken words. Our words can create or destroy as well.

Dear Lord, forgive my harsh and judgmental words about myself and others. I have no right to discredit the person You have created. Help me to see myself and others as You do. Grant me patience and self-control when anger wants to explode. It might be righteous anger, but I recognize it's not the person but the spirit behind the person's words or actions. Teach me to hold my tongue and wait for Your inspiration. Likewise, help me to acknowledge others with encouraging words.

Today I will find ways to bless myself
and others with kind words.

My Walk

MARCH 4

Happy are those who hear the joyful call to worship,
for they will walk in the light of your presence, LORD.
Psalm 89:15, NLT

We've come a long way, haven't we? As baby Christians, there was so much to grasp. Like toddlers learning to walk, we stumbled occasionally. The gospel message began to transform your nature as you spent more time with other believers, read His Word, and heard anointed messages. Even as mature Christians, you might still battle with the old nature. You've learned a thing or two: I'm not perfect, but I keep walking!

Oh Lord, I think back to my early days with You. You were (and still are) so kind and comforting, always there to nudge me back on track when I stepped out of line. My old nature still surfaces now and then. I trust You with my heart motives and emotions. Help me to stop, look, and listen to Holy Spirit whenever I'm confused about my next step.

Today I will march forth and follow in Your steps.

Heal My Hurts

MARCH 5

The LORD is close to the brokenhearted
and saves those who are crushed in spirit.
Psalm 34:18, NIV

Hurts, offenses, disappointments, and crushed dreams can break your heart. Self-protection against further damage can prevent you from trying again or believing that things could change. But the love and wisdom of God are constantly knocking on your heart, asking you to open up to His healing touch. You can just sit, stew, and wallow in self-pity. Or you can take your wounds to the cross and walk through with Jesus to the other side of victory. Pray, forgive, love, and live again!

Lord, only You know the scream that's inside of me. You heard those hurtful words. You saw my face and my tears. You felt the arrows that hit my heart. You also know my faults and my blame. Help me now to let go of these hurtful things. I want to be free of any memory that keeps me from a joyful heart. Heal me and bandage my wounds, Jesus.

Today I will be set free from a broken heart.

The Prickles

Saul, Saul, why do you persecute me?
It is hard for you to kick against the goads.
Acts 26:14, NIV

The word "goad" can also mean a prick, a sting, or a sharp point.[1]
We are so fortunate to have Holy Spirit as our constant companion.
How many times have you felt that prick in your conscience? *Oops!*
I shouldn't have said that. I wish I hadn't done that. Why did I give
in to that? Saul's encounter with Jesus later transformed him into
Paul, the most prolific writer of the New Testament. Giving your
heart to the Lord teaches you to gladly yield to His goads.

Lord, I want to tell You how thankful I am that You came into my
life. I love how You give me that check in my spirit not to follow my
wrong instincts but to yield to Yours. I know I'm a work in
progress. I don't take any credit except for trying as I am able.
Thanks for being my enabler!

Today I will be sensitive to Holy Spirit prickles.

Trauma Free

Who will separate us from the love of Christ?
Will tribulation, or trouble, or persecution, or famine,
or nakedness, or danger, or sword?
Romans 8:35, NASB

As beloved Christ-followers, we can give *and* receive remedies for trauma. It can be a Band-Aid for the body, an "I'm sorry" for the soul, or an encouraging word for the spirit. We can receive and be the cure for brokenness. How? Through Christ! Why? Because the Father first loved you[1] and sent His Son for you. You can love yourself and others through absolutely anything when you grasp the absolute truth of His eternal love.

Father, thank You for Your plan of salvation through Your Son, Jesus. Holy Spirit loved me so much that He drew me to Jesus and His message of salvation. I can't imagine going through trials and troubles without You. You are my source of comfort, renewal, and freedom. If anything left in me from the past needs uprooting, show me now. I trust in Your love to pull it out.

Today the love of Christ will set me truly free.

Forgiveness

MARCH 8

And when you stand praying, if you hold anything
against anyone, forgive them, so that your Father
in heaven may forgive you your sins.
Mark 11:25, NIV

We've heard stories about prisoners who forgave their jailors,
families who forgave the drunken driver, and other such stories. A
classic favorite in the Bible is Joseph and his brothers, who sold him
into slavery and lied to their father. Joseph's famous line in Genesis
50:20 (NASB) was, *"You meant evil against me, but God meant it*
for good." And then there's Job and his so-called friends. In both
stories, Joseph and Job forgave and reaped the rewards.

Father, I don't want any hindrance to having my prayers answered.
Please show me if there is any situation in my life where I hold
unforgiveness. I come before You now with my heart open. Show me
if I have any bitterness or resentment toward anyone. I choose to
forgive them now. I set them free. Now, set me free. I close the door
and give You the key.

Today, show me if I have any unforgiveness in my heart.

Cleanse Me

Now you have been purified from sin, made holy,
and given a perfect standing before God—all because of
the power of the name of the Lord Jesus, the Messiah,
and through our union with the Spirit of our God.
1 Corinthians 6:11, TPT

Rust-colored water from the tap indicates there is corrosion in the water pipes. You can't see the effect of deterioration until the damage is obvious. The same is true of the river of life that flows within you. With salvation, you are washed clean and made new. Sometimes, your old nature creeps in, so you may need another dip. God delights in wiping the smudge and tears from your face.

Lord Jesus, I know I've slipped a bit in the past and maybe even now. I delight in Your presence and am so grateful for what You've done for me. I choose to spend time with You today. Remove the rust and clean out the impurities, Holy Spirit. I need Your cleansing touch. Let Your river of life flow in me.

Today I bathe myself in Your presence,
and I will be clean.

Right Side Up

I have told you these things, so that in me you
may have peace. In this world you will have trouble.
But take heart! I have overcome the world.
John 16:33, NIV

In this topsy-turvy world, up is down, and down is up. Haven't you felt that way? You try to jump over hurdles, but you don't have the juice sometimes. Think of the turtle in his hard shell. Flat on his back with feet flailing, he needs a gentle push. Maybe you do too. Take courage, grab Jesus's hand, and let Him lift you up and over.

Thank You, Jesus, for Your words. Your stories and instructions show me that You understand what it is to be human. I try so hard. I sometimes take things into my own hands and try to make things right. Other times, I'm so weary of trying, and I give up. I bring these hurdles to You today. Give me wisdom, encourage my heart, and help me overcome.

Today I will have peace and courage
as Jesus helps me overcome.

Little by Little

MARCH 11

*The LORD your God will drive out those nations before you,
little by little. You will not be allowed to eliminate them all
at once, or the wild animals will multiply around you.*
Deuteronomy 7:22, NIV

Over time, any repeated action or substance could harm us. You
may only recognize the danger once you face the results. It's like
the frog in the pot with the gradual heat increase. The same is true
in deliverance from past hurt and trauma. The Lord is gracious and
kind. He's the God of perfection and has wisdom to lead you to
freedom gently and fully in His time.

*Lord, You and I both know I must address certain issues that harm
me and those I love. Protect me from further damage to myself and
others. I trust Your tender touch. Coach me along the way. Prepare
my heart for victory. Soften me where I've been hard-hearted. Heal
me where I've been brokenhearted.*

**Today I will put my heart in the Lord's
hand and wait for Him.**

Relief

MARCH 12

Answer me when I call to you, my righteous God.
Give me relief from my distress; have mercy
on me and hear my prayer.
Psalm 4:1, NIV

Our eyes, throats, lungs, and skin are easily irritated when we come into contact with something foreign to our bodies. In the same way, your soul and spirit can also have an adverse reaction to irritation. The Lord is always mindful of your needs. Sometimes, you are being tested. Other times, the enemy is attacking your weakness. At all times, you can appeal to the Lord in prayer. He's waiting for you to call out to Him today.

It doesn't matter if it's minor or major distress, Lord. I am so grateful that You hear me when I call to You. Even when I don't have an immediate answer, I trust You. Thank You for Your Word that comforts me and gives me the courage to wait in faith for Your answer. In the in-between time, Lord, could You wash over me with Your peace and presence? Thank You for Your mercy.

Today I am relieved that the Lord
always hears my prayers.

Bandages

MARCH 13

I will search for my lost ones who strayed away,
and I will bring them safely home again.
I will bandage the injured and strengthen the weak.
Ezekiel 34:16, NLT

Wound care for the body is similar to wound care for the soul and spirit. Dressings need to be changed daily with proper healing ointment. They need moisture and protection. Removing the scab too soon can result in a scar. So it is with our Lord. He knows when you've been wounded, and the Father knows how to care for His children with the precious blood of His Son and the refreshing wind of His Spirit.

Father, I can't tell You how much it means to know that You will never forsake or leave me. When I come to You like this in prayer, I feel Your presence and Your sweet comfort. Can we just stay like this for a while? I need Your healing touch to bandage my wounds.

Today I will feel the Lord touch my wounds
and strengthen my spirit and soul.

Mountains to Molehills

Who are you, O great mountain? Before Zerubbabel
you shall become a plain. And he shall bring forward
the top stone amid shouts of "Grace, grace to it!"
Zechariah 4:7, ESV

Have you ever experienced a conversation or a situation that exploded out of control? Most of us have. Miscommunication and misunderstanding are at the root of many relationship issues. Repeated hurts and slight offenses signal something deeper might be going on. Our first reaction might be self-*right*-eousness. How might the peacemaker, Jesus, call you to model His grace? Be the first to humble yourself in conflict with another.

Lord, some situations in my life are complicated. I'm not at fault for some of them. Others, well, You know I had a part to play. Could You help me find a way through? I want to make a fresh start. Forgive me for harboring offense. I'm sorry, Lord, for making a mountain out of a molehill. With Your grace and forgiveness, help me make molehills out of these mountains.

**Today I will take positive steps to resolve
relationship issues with God's grace.**

A New Identity

*Could it be any clearer that our former identity is now
and forever deprived of its power? For we were
co-crucified with him to dismantle the stronghold of sin
within us, so that we would not continue to live one
moment longer submitted to sin's power.*
Romans 6:6, TPT

Have you believed the lie about you? Most of us have at some point. Sometimes, those lies are ingrained as early as childhood. They lay hidden at the root of our self-talk and insecurities. The accuser delights in getting us off-track from our real identities and purposes. It's time for a reroute and a reboot.

Jesus, thank You for this day of freedom. Because of You, I can shut the door on the enemy's lies. You love me, You are for me, and You made a way for me to step into my true identity in You. Thank You, Holy Spirit, for shining the light on those hidden things. I love being on the right track with You.

Today I will face the lies and shout, "No more!"

Know My Heart

MARCH 16

Each heart knows its own bitterness,
and no one else can fully share its joy.
Proverbs 14:10, NLT

When it comes down to it, we are stand-alone people. Yes, you have family, friends, and coworkers, even best friends. But truth be told, you are an island in a sea of people. No one knows your hidden scream, your longing, your hurt, or the pain you hide. Similarly, no one understands your delights, favorites, or soft spots. But God the Father does. He knows you inside and out and loves you just the way you are. Sure, there may be some tweaks, but time is on His side.

Father, I look in the mirror and only see my reflection. You look at me and see right through. I wish I could be as transparent with myself. Sometimes, I confuse myself and wonder who I am and what I should feel. I rejoice in knowing that You love me just as I am. Help me to be the person You know I can be.

Today I will trust the Lord with my heart.

Nothing Is Wasted

MARCH 17

And we know that all things work together
for good to those who love God, to those who are
the called according to His *purpose.*
Romans 8:28, NKJV

Time, tears, trials. Sunrises, sunsets, sorrow. Learning, loving, living. Life experiences build character and fortify you for future expected and unexpected events. Unfortunately, you can get caught up in the day's challenge, pulled in every direction. Instead of looking back with regret or at today's test, look forward. There's a book about you in heaven. Really! See Psalm 139:16. Ask the Lord to show you the next page for today's purpose.

Lord, I'm pulled every which way with responsibilities. Some days, I feel so depleted. Today, I just need some quiet time with You. Help me to see Your purpose in all that's drawing on my energy and focus. You've called me for such a time as this. So, I trust that You know what You're doing in my life. Help me see what You have planned for me in the natural and the spiritual realms.

Today the Lord will show me His plan
and purpose for my day.

Barriers

MARCH 18

For he himself is our peace, who has made
the two groups one and has destroyed the barrier,
the dividing wall of hostility.
Ephesians 2:14, NIV

Unforgiveness, carrying an offense, pride, and division are obstacles that can impede our progress. Jesus obliterates these barriers with one word: "Peace!" You might say, "Well, that's Jesus." Yes, that's true. But as He is, so are you. Everything is possible when you let Jesus be the bridge between you and the obstacle. There is no barrier when you allow God's love, the cross's power, and Holy Spirit's flow to make a way.

Lord, today is the day. I want to bring a couple of things to Your attention. I know I have some unfinished business with barriers I have allowed. My heart tells me so. I am willing to have You address these issues. Show me where to admit my part and then how to pray for the other side. Soften both hearts with Your peace. Take my hand, and walk me across the bridge to freedom. Help me break through the obstacles.

Today I will tear down the barriers
I have erected.

Desert Blooms

MARCH 19

The wilderness and dry land will be joyously glad!
The desert will blossom like a rose and rejoice!
Isaiah 35:1, TPT

The wilderness experience is barren and seems to last forever. It might be an illness, a dead-end job, taking care of a sick parent, or housing children after they should be on their own. Whatever the challenge, for those of us who know the Lord, He is with us. His grace develops your courage and endurance. His love covers a multitude of wishes. His mercy can fill you with hope for your situation. His joy will become your joy. Be on the lookout. The rain is coming, and you will blossom again.

Lord, my situation hasn't changed. I'm still struggling with frustration and delay. At least my attitude has changed. What would I do without Your encouragement? Thank You for the peace in my heart, the anxiety off my shoulders, and the sleep I enjoy at night. Every morning is a new day to live in Your promises. I trust You with my tomorrows.

**Today I will rejoice that God
provides in the desert.**

Motion Detectors

MARCH 20

Be alert and of sober mind.
Your enemy the devil prowls around like
a roaring lion looking for someone to devour.
1 Peter 5:8, NIV

Holy Spirit is like a motion detector. He nudges us and sheds light on situations that might cause harm. He knows just how to get our attention and alert us to danger. Do you listen? How many times have you felt a nudge just before leaving the house? *Check the coffee pot. Is the door locked? Do you have your phone?* Or, *Call Mom. Send a note. Text a friend.* Or, *Don't say it; stop right there. Speak up.* Ask Him to amp it up until you get used to His alerts.

Holy Spirit, You are my best friend. I love how You watch my every move. Thank You for walking beside me every day. Your wisdom guides my words and actions. You detect my moods and offer gentle reminders. Your nudges help me so often. Your timing is perfect. I don't mind it when You poke me. But sometimes, I wish You'd talk a little louder.

Today I will be sensitive to Holy Spirit
pokes, jabs, and nudges.

New Garments

*Let us draw near to God with a sincere heart and with
the full assurance that faith brings, having our hearts
sprinkled to cleanse us from a guilty conscience
and having our bodies washed with pure water.*
Hebrews 10:22, NIV

The Lord is so amazing. Here we are, sinners, yet He drew us to His heart with His message of love and salvation. We exchanged our filthy rags for garments of light. Sure, it takes time for the fullness of that transformation to take effect, but every step is a major milestone to be more like Jesus. The old *me* is passing away as the new *me* is forming.

Thank You, Jesus, for giving Your body and precious blood as a sacrifice for my life. Day by day and year by year, I sense a remarkable change in me. The things that were so important are strangely dim now. I don't need them as much as I need You. And, Lord, I can't wait to see what You will do next in my life.

Today I will put on the garment of praise.

Constriction

MARCH 22

Strive to enter through the narrow door.
For many, I tell you, will seek to enter and will not be able.
Luke 13:24, ESV

Internal pressure builds when there is constriction, which can be a good thing as long as it doesn't explode. We recognize that warning touch from Holy Spirit. He transforms us from glory to glory. Long-held habits don't seem compatible with the life you want to lead. The Greek word for "strive" actually means to contend for a prize.[1] Just imagine the rewards waiting for you when you let these things go.

Lord, I've got a lifetime of habits I know I need to address. Even after walking with You this long, I still get disappointed in myself. I sense Holy Spirit's finger poking me, but I need Your grace. Help me to come face-to-face with this pressure. I want to be free. I know a reward is on the other side. Fight for me, Jesus, as I contend for the prize.

Today the Lord will pinpoint where
there is grace for change.

Liberate Me

MARCH 23

Now the Lord is that Spirit:
and where the Spirit of the Lord is, there is liberty.
2 Corinthians 3:17, KJV

Disagreement ties two parties in bondage. Sometimes, we are in the right but have to let go. And sometimes, it's the other party that has to let go. It could be arguments, painful words, or wrong judgments. So who is going to let go first? It all depends, doesn't it? What we forget is Jesus said to turn the other cheek.[1] When you do, the Lord, our conqueror, can enter into the battle. And He never loses.

Lord, sometimes it's tough to give in to an argument when I know I'm right, but the other person won't budge. I feel tied up in knots. I want to let Your grace guide me. Help me maintain a spirit of peace and reconciliation. Give me inspiration on how to approach them. I invite You into the middle of every unresolved situation. Your Spirit will guide us both into the freedom and liberty that forgiveness brings.

Today the Spirit of peace will instruct
me and set me free.

Challenge the Lie

MARCH 24

Beloved, do not believe every spirit,
but test the spirits to see whether they are from God.
1 John 4:1, BSB

Our enemy is very good at lying and using what others say to hurt us—"You're not good enough." "You'll never be free." "That situation will never change." "You might as well give up." Or maybe we've believed the enemy's lies, and we experience negative self-talk—"I blew it again." "I'll never succeed." "She's so much better than me." "I can't do it." The enemy of your soul is always at work, twisting, turning, and challenging your faith. Sometimes, it's your own words that feed failure. Put that lie to the test. Ask God about who you really are and listen to Him.

Spirit of truth, You know everything, even hidden lies that hold me back. Reveal the deception I have believed. Show me where false words have taken root and flourished. Highlight the lies I believe about myself. I want to be free from any hindrance that keeps me from the fullness of my destiny with You.

Today I call out the lie and face it
with truth and grace.

Appease or Displease?

If any of you lacks wisdom, you should ask God,
who gives generously to all without finding fault,
and it will be given to you.
James 1:5, NIV

Do we feed the lamb or the lion? Good question! When chaos surrounds us, we often want peace at any price. There's a price to pay when you yield to avoidance and convenience. Matters are never really settled, just delayed for the next battle. Our God *is* wisdom. He knows you inside and out. In this case, you feed the lamb and surrender your need to God. When you have His answer, you feed the lion and stand your ground.

Lord, I am thankful I can bring my battles to You and Your Word. You set my heart at ease and give me strategies to approach challenges. You are teaching and training me to become an excellent warrior. Fill me with Your grace and wisdom. Show me the way through. I won't back away. I will follow in Your steps.

Today I will be both a lamb and a lion.

Influencers

MARCH 26

You were running a good race.
Who cut in on you to keep you from obeying the truth?
Galatians 5:7, NIV

Like most, we all set goals. We even start with great intentions, but then we fizzle. Your goals might be to change your diet, read the Word every day, prioritize date nights, go on walks, or something similar. What changed? Often, it's distractions and outside influence. Take some quiet time with the Lord and ask Him for revelation. Don't be surprised by the forces standing in the way of the finish line. The enemy of your success is always actively engaged. But *you* have the Spirit of truth running beside you!

Thank You, God, that You see the race I am running and know the hurdles I face. I need Your wisdom and guidance to see the roadblocks and learn how to maneuver around them. Alert me when there is an outside influence, whether from today's culture, the voices I listen to, or when I intentionally veer off the path. Keep me on track with You.

Today I will run my race successfully
as I listen and obey the Spirit of truth.

Let Them Go

MARCH 27

Flee the evil desires of youth and pursue righteousness,
faith, love and peace, along with those who call
on the Lord out of a pure heart.
2 Timothy 2:22, NIV

Sometimes, we need to take stock of who is around us. Be honest. It's hard to walk away from longtime friends who aren't a positive influence. The Lord's goodness in you always wants to see good and do good. Joy-stealers put a drain on your mental and emotional resources. Some may even tempt you to return to your old life. There may come a time when the Lord says, "Walk away but pray."

Oh Lord, something keeps coming up in my spirit about my friend. I have tried to live my Christian life out loud with them. I'm not pushy or preachy. I've left that old lifestyle for good, and my spirit comes alive when I'm with other believers. Help me rebuff temptation and strive for purity, especially in my relationships.

Today I will bring my friends before
the Lord and listen.

Only a Reflection

MARCH 28

For now we see only a reflection as in a mirror;
then we shall see face to face. Now I know in part;
then I shall know fully, even as I am fully known.
1 Corinthians 13:12, NIV

Don't ever lose sight of your progress. Walking with the Lord day-by-day, month-by-month, and year-by-year is a process. You will never be perfect until the day when you see Jesus face-to-face. All these tests and trials will be over in the twinkling of an eye. That should bring you the most remarkable hope.

Jesus, You are the bright morning star. Someday, I will stand before You and behold Your brilliance. How I long to look into Your eyes. You went to the cross long before I was born, but You knew me even then. You've watched me from my youth. You've seen me through my adulthood phases. Today, You see me just as I am. I'm not perfect, but I'm so in love with You.

Today I will praise You, Jesus, for
Your victories in my life.

Made New

Now, if anyone is enfolded into Christ, he has become
an entirely new person. All that is related to the old order
has vanished. Behold, everything is fresh and new.
2 Corinthians 5:17, TPT

You've heard it said, "If nothing ever changed, there would be no butterflies." Before we meet Jesus, we are like caterpillars stuck in ugly bodies. After your new life begins, you feed on His love and His Word. Holy Spirit cocoons your spirit. Transformation begins in the secret place hidden in Him. You fully emerge when you discover who you are *in* Christ and who He is in you.

Jesus, change is hard. Some days are more challenging than others,
and disappointment often knocks at the door of my heart. Holy
Spirit, I need Your help. I could use some patience and long
suffering today. Have I made any progress? Show me something
fresh and new about me. I so want to be like You, Jesus.

Today I will remember how far I've come
since Jesus came into my life.

A Contrite Heart

*I live in the high and holy place with those whose spirits
are contrite and humble. I restore the crushed spirit of the humble
and revive the courage of those with repentant hearts.*
Isaiah 57:15, NLT

Our Father is enthroned in heaven and in our hearts. He longs for a
relationship with you, but He is *holy*. Sin and pride can get in the
way. Your breakthrough comes when you recognize sin and humble
yourself to ask forgiveness. You look up to Him as He looks down
to you. Love and blessing meet in the middle as you soften under
His gaze. The Father loves humility. What would you like to say to
Him today?

*Thank You, Jesus, for restoring my relationship with the Father. He
is high and lifted up in my heart, but I sometimes don't feel good
enough in my thoughts. I begin each day with good intentions, but
my pride can get the best of me. I trust You and Holy Spirit to
help me.*

**Today I will feel the Father's smile
when I yield to Him.**

Fountain of Life

MARCH 31

The fountain of life flows from you to satisfy me.
In your light of holiness we receive the light of revelation.
Psalm 36:9, TPT

We don't know what we don't know. That's why we need an intimate relationship with the Lord. The right time seems to be everything with Him. Have you ever had an issue you've struggled with resolve instantly? It could be a revelation while reading His Word, a conversation with another believer, or an anointed message from the pulpit. But the Lord always reveals the answer at the right time.

Thank You, Lord, for keeping me under the shadow of Your wing. My tendency is to be disappointed in myself and my situation. But when I spend time with You, I am filled with light and hope. You open my heart to hear Your counsel. I feel Your presence, and You wash me in Your fountain of love.

Today I will be renewed in His fountain of life.

April

WHAT NEEDS TO MAKE ROOM FOR NEW?

Just as the natural world revives after winter's hibernation, your dormant gifts and dreams emerge as you embrace your identity in Christ. It's time to go the extra mile. Spring cleaning is thorough and includes your firm decision to throw out the old to make room for the new.

Once you have determined your true identity and the lies that bind you, you can establish a new approach to daily faith-filled living. It begins with His truth and progresses to commitment and action on what you've experienced. How? By agreeing in faith with His Word and through your declarations.

This month, your prayers and declarations will gain firepower as you advance with Holy Spirit's help into deeper waters. God knows your challenges, but He also knows you'll experience breakthroughs this month. So get out your broom, sweep those cobwebs away, and freshen your outlook. It's going to be a bright and shiny spring. Expect resurrection power to infuse your thinking and your actions.

Search and Find

Or suppose a woman has ten silver coins and loses one.
Doesn't she light a lamp, sweep the house and
search carefully until she finds it?
Luke 15:8, NIV

Jesus's Parable of the Lost Coin is apt for some of us. In our deepest parts, we know the Lord has put an unfulfilled desire in our hearts. Family responsibilities, your workload, or maybe health has kept you from pursuing that deep longing. That dream seed in you needs to be watered. Let Holy Spirit pull your hat box off the closet shelf. Open it up, look inside, and put it on.

I'm feeling a bit timid about this, Lord. Do You remember that idea You put in my heart so long ago? I want to talk to You about it today. You gave it to me for a reason, and I want to bring it up again. How can we work on this together? Forgive me for thinking I wasn't good enough. It's not me. It's You in me.

Today I will dream with the Lord.

My Broom Closet

The secret things belong to the LORD our God,
but the things revealed belong to us
and to our children forever.
Deuteronomy 29:29, NIV

Some of us have very organized broom or storage closets. Others are over-stuffed. Dreams and ideas can be like that. Think of your quiet time with Holy Spirit as being in a prayer broom closet. He'll likely show you some areas where deep scratches (wounds) in your heart need wood filler (the cross). Maybe there's a wax buildup (unbelief) on your foundation (truths), requiring some stripping (cleansing). Let Him shine His light on your hidden areas that need His loving touch.

Lord, sitting in this prayer broom closet is uncomfortable but necessary. I look forward to sorting things out with You. As I take inventory of my life and set things in Your order, I'm beginning to see the possibilities. Thank You for revealing Your secret passion for me. You encourage me to examine the whole picture and recognize where to start dreaming again.

Today I will strategize with the Lord.

Work-Arounds

*Seek his will in all you do, and he will
show you which path to take.*
Proverbs 3:6, NLT

We all face genuine problems that need answers. The easy way is usually only a temporary fix. Those answers can be creative and outside the box, but you'll eventually need a permanent solution. The Lord *is* wisdom! He knows the pressures you face and what's on your plate. You can attempt to resolve issues independently or take the winning route. Why don't you sit down with the Lord and let Him sort it out?

Lord, I've got a few challenges on my plate today. You see my workload. You hear the disagreements. You sense my disquiet trying to be a peacemaker and problem-solver. That's why I surely need Your input today. As I bring each of these to Your attention, quicken my heart for the best path and priority. I could use some good ideas. No, actually, I could use Your *best ideas.*

**Today I will discover a real solution to a real
problem, in Jesus's name!**

Jump Start

APRIL 4

The soul of the sluggard craves and gets nothing,
while the soul of the diligent is richly supplied.
Proverbs 13:4, ESV

Remember when you were a child, and your parents coaxed you with "Don't dawdle" or "Stop dilly-dallying"? Well, our Eternal Father just might feel the same. In your heart, you surely remember something the Lord told you to do, and you haven't done it. Maybe you brushed it off with, "That can't be God." Or you felt ill-equipped to do the job. The Father is calling you back to move forward in His plan and purpose. He's ready to reignite the flame in you!

So, Lord, You know that thing You talked to me about so long ago? Could we talk about it again? Forgive me for putting so many other attention-getters ahead of Yours. I need to redirect my focus at this point in my life. Meet me here in this quiet place. I'm not in a hurry, and I promise I won't drag my feet. Stir my soul and spirit once again.

Today I will be diligent and faithful to His call.

A Clear Vision

"For I know the plans I have for you,"
declares the LORD, "plans to prosper you and
not to harm you, plans to give you hope and a future."
Jeremiah 29:11, NIV

Decision-making is always challenging. It's hard to focus on the big picture or the desired outcome with all the ifs, ands, or buts yelling at you. The Lord doesn't want you confused and going every which way. He wants you focused and moving toward that end goal. So why don't you clear away the distractions, find that quiet space, get out your pad and pen, and write the vision with Him?

As a child, I loved to draw pictures of things I imagined. Today, Lord, I want to draw with You. I know there's something extraordinary that You've planned for my life. I need Your help navigating all of these current pulls. I seem to be going in all sorts of directions. Perhaps I've taken on more than I should? Bring clarity to Your plans for me.

Today I will have a clear vision
of the Lord's plans.

Maximize Me

APRIL 6

*Then Isaac sowed in that land, and reaped in the same
year a hundredfold; and the LORD blessed him.*
Genesis 26:12, NKJV

Remember the story of Isaac when there was a famine in the land?
Isaac wanted to leave, but the Lord told him to stay and plant crops.
Because of his obedience, Isaac harvested a hundred times what
he'd planted. We recognize the principle of sowing and reaping.
Spring is the perfect time for super-sized faith. The Father has great
plans for you. Let Him show you how to get there.

*Father, Isaiah 55:8 says that Your ways are not my ways. Isaac's
story is proof of that. What You told him to do didn't make sense to
the natural mind. But to You, who guided him and had his best
interests at heart, it was a miraculous plan. I know there is a God-
sized purpose in me that hasn't reached fullness. Help me uncover
it and obey You in whatever You've called me to do.*

Today I will seek the Lord for His plans for me.

Time to Declutter

Forget the former things; do not dwell on the past.
See, I am doing a new thing! Now it springs up;
do you not perceive it? I am making a way in the
wilderness and streams in the wasteland.
Isaiah 43:18–19, NIV

Clutter begins small and builds over time. Distractions and disorder immobilize and overwhelm us under their confusion. So, where do you begin? You start at the top surface when you clean your house and work your way down. The same decluttering principle applies to what the Lord calls you to initiate. It all becomes clear when you put your eyes and heart on Him alone. Ask the Lord to show you the new thing and His new way.

I have no more excuses, Lord. I've felt Your nudge, but I feel inadequate. There are so many responsibilities on my plate. It seems everyone needs me. But, Lord, You do too. I'm going to look to You for inspiration. You are my top priority. Help me deal with the things that hold me back. Show me Your way.

Today I will clear my mind of clutter
and see His way.

Light Beams

APRIL 8

You will also declare a thing, And it will be established
for you; So light will shine on your ways.
Job 22:28, NKJV

When we start fresh at something new, it's like a toddler learning to walk. At first, we are a little wobbly, but we see the goal in sight. No matter what, we keep getting up and trying again. What you think and what you speak are so very important. When the Lord shines His light on an area of your life, He's there for you. You say what He says because you've got His Word on it! What is the Lord saying to you?

So here we are, Lord. I'm going to make that fresh start we talked about. You wouldn't have dropped it into my heart if You weren't planning on shining Your light on it. Thank You for Your encouragement. Help me to see the path forward. I promise to walk in Your footsteps as I make these daily declarations. Beam on, Holy Spirit!

Today I will see the light ahead,
speak to it, and follow it.

Special Treasure

APRIL 9

Now if you will obey me and keep my covenant,
you will be my own special treasure from among all the
peoples on earth; for all the earth belongs to me.
Exodus 19:5, NLT

Obedience brings its reward. We are people who understand the call of duty to God and others. Integrity and the values you hold dear compel you to put them first. But don't forget that the sacrifices you make for others do not go unnoticed. God rewards the diligent. Think of it this way. You have a treasure chest in heaven. Why not make a withdrawal? Step out in faith and do what He's called you to do.

Lord, I delight in hearing from You and obeying You. I don't regret the responsibilities You've entrusted to me. I'm grateful for my energy and abilities. Sometimes, I feel caught up in all my to-dos and have little time left over. I have dreams I want to pursue with You. Could we open up my treasure chest today?

Today I will ask the Lord for a glimpse
of heaven on earth.

Resilience

APRIL 10

Do not grieve, for the joy of the LORD is your strength.
Nehemiah 8:10, NIV

How do we bounce back from difficulties? We encourage ourselves like David with song and praise, and the joy of the Lord begins to bubble up again. You can get down in the dumps over just about anything that taxes your soul if you let it. That's the key phrase: let it. You have a firm foundation in the Lord. You know where your strength lies when the winds blow and storms brew. The Lord is your refuge and strong tower. You just have to run to Him. He's waiting for you with open arms.

I am so grateful for worship music, Lord. When I get down and circumstances seem to pile up on me, all I have to do is put on some music and praise You. How amazing that You made Your children like this! I can face any challenge with You by my side. Thank You for the song in my heart. You are my joy.

Today I will rejoice in the Lord, and He will strengthen me.

Brick Walls

With your help I can advance against a troop;
with my God I can scale a wall.
2 Samuel 22:30, NIV

Insurmountable challenges require a heart-strong attitude. There's the unending battle we have with our flesh; then there's family or coworkers, and we always have the outside influence of the enemy of our progress. But God! If you want a fresh start and to break through that brick wall, you must know that Almighty God is on your side. What do you do? You take a leap of faith. If necessary, you can dismantle that wall brick by brick with the promises of God.

Oh Lord, You are mighty and strong in battle. You are my champion. You are always for me and even go before me in advance of what You've called me to do. Brick walls are nothing for Your might, but they are real to me. I lean on You for wisdom and revelation. Show me the direction and strategy for these challenges.

Today I will strengthen my heart
with the promises of God.

Begin Agains

APRIL 12

The Lord isn't really being slow about his promise,
as some people think. No, he is being patient for your sake.
2 Peter 3:9, NLT

Aren't you glad our God is in favor of do-overs? Our modern world gives us delete buttons, backspaces, and correction tape to cut out or cover our mistakes. We have the precious blood of Jesus. Starting over feels so good when you correct your errors and run to Him. The Lord's patient heart grants you mercy and grace when you admit you are wrong. Would you like to begin again in a particular area? He's already waiting for you there.

What would I do without You, Holy Spirit? Thank You for constantly checking my heart and giving me a nudge when I'm out of step with You and kingdom principles. You are gentle and kind and quicken my soul when I'm off the mark. I am so grateful. This spring, I want to go on a new adventure with You as I pursue Your purpose for my life.

Today I will begin again with a can-do attitude.

Enthusiasm

APRIL 13

But we who live by the Spirit eagerly wait to receive by
faith the righteousness God has promised to us.
Galatians 5:5, NLT

When we eagerly desire something, we pursue it with gusto. The spark of what *can be* motivates our hearts, minds, and even our feet. Doubt and timidity will always quench your spirit and let fear take hold. But when it's a God-dream, nothing can stop you. If you've heard from God, then you can bank on it. You have the blessed presence of Holy Spirit anytime you need Him. Go ahead. Just ask. By faith, you know His answer is coming.

Thank You, Lord, for this fire growing inside of me. You are blowing on the flame of possibilities. My spirit is curious, excited, and even a little impatient. Prepare me for what's ahead. Your Word and promises direct my desires, decisions, and steps. I yield to Your timing, but I also want You to know I'm excited to get started.

Today I will fan the flame of faith
and wait patiently.

A New Day

APRIL 14

The faithful love of the LORD never ends!
His mercies never cease. Great is his faithfulness;
his mercies begin afresh each morning.
Lamentations 3:22–23, NLT

We all experience life's storms where darkness creeps in, confusion swirls, and we feel helpless. But when the new day dawns, hope surges, possibilities begin to take shape, and light shines in the darkness. That's the rebounding love of the Father, Son, and Holy Spirit. How could you ever doubt His power and promises? On this journey, let faith flood your heart today. Let your hope rise with the sun each morning.

Lord, I sometimes have restless nights where the worries of the day before compete with my much-needed sleep. As I spend time with You today, I lift each one off my shoulder and onto Yours. Jesus, You said in Matthew 11:30 that Your yoke was easy. Thank You for taking mine. I want to start this day drenched in Your sunshine. Thank You for Your faithfulness to me. Help me to be faithful to You.

Today I will have joy in my heart
and energy in my step.

Our Helper

*And I will pray the Father, and He will give you
another Helper, that He may abide with you forever—the
Spirit of truth, whom the world cannot receive, because it
neither sees Him nor knows Him; but you know Him,
for He dwells with you and will be in you.*
John 14:16–17, NKJV

As we make progress this spring, be encouraged that you are not alone. Jesus promised us that the Father would send Holy Spirit and the Spirit of truth would dwell within us. We are such a peculiar people. The world doesn't understand you, but Holy Spirit does. Your faithful companion, teacher, and motivator will be with you every step of the way, guiding you by His truth.

*Holy Spirit, thank You for being my constant friend and companion.
I honor Your presence in my life. I love how You drop people into
my heart for prayer or to make contact. I'm becoming more
sensitive to Your nudges. Thank You for making my heart smile.
What's next for today?*

**Today I will act on what Holy Spirit
puts on my heart.**

A Little TLC

*I will forever praise this God who didn't close his heart
when I prayed and never said no when I asked him for
help. He never once refused to show me his tender love.*
Psalm 66:20, TPT

Sometimes, we feel overwhelmed by all the pulls on our energy and stamina. In times like these, most of us escape to our quiet place. It may be a back patio, a walk, a car ride, or into your closet and closing the door. That's where you meet your problem solver and peace maker. You need this alone time as you negotiate change and God's dreams in your heart. He's looking for some me-time with you!

*Lord, I'm trying hard to please everyone, but I feel like I come up
short now and then. Today, I'm reaching out to You to refill the well
of hope and purpose in my life. I need some tender, loving care
from You. Refresh me in this quiet time. Redirect my thinking, and
restore my soul.*

**Today I will receive and be refreshed
by the Lord's TLC.**

In Training

For the moment, all discipline seems not to be pleasant,
but painful; yet to those who have been trained by it, afterward it
yields the peaceful fruit of righteousness.
Hebrews 12:11, NASB

How often do we hear the encouraging phrase, "No pain, no gain"? It's a hard and fast rule of life. To reach a goal, we must continually press in and press on. Fortunately for us, we have the best training coach ever! The indwelling Holy Spirit constantly encourages you along His path of purpose for your life. Keep your eyes on the prize He's dropped into your heart. Coach is blowing His whistle for you now.

I know You've put this thought in my heart, Lord. It won't go away.
I feel Your encouragement to get moving in the right direction. I'm
ready to commit my time and effort. I can't do this without Your
help. I give You permission to correct me whenever I step out of
line or drop to the back of the line. I know You have great plans
for me.

Today I'm in it to win it.

All In

APRIL 18

Remember this: Whoever sows sparingly
will also reap sparingly, and whoever sows
generously will also reap generously.
2 Corinthians 9:6, NIV

The Lord is gracious to us and abundantly supplies gifts, talents, and even genius abilities. Some of us may have difficulty spelling, and others may not be too coordinated. But count on the truth that you are uniquely qualified to accomplish God's purpose for your life. The key to your success is first, believing what He's put in your heart, and second, committing to giving it your all-in-all. So, what has the Lord put in your heart? Are you all in?

Lord, I could give up, give out, or give in. I choose to give it my all. This seed You've planted in my heart needs what only You can provide. Nourish my soul with Your confidence, breathe on my spirit with Your revelation, and energize my body with Your power. I choose to plant all the seeds You've given me. I won't hold back. I'm all Yours. I'm all in.

Today I am all in, and I will sow
generously into my future.

Under Pressure

And do not be conformed to this world, but be transformed
by the renewing of your mind, that you may prove what is
that good and acceptable and perfect will of God.
Romans 12:2, NKJV

What keeps you from pursuing the *me* God made you to be? It could be personal pressures like workload, time constraints, or circumstances beyond your control. It could be external pressures in our society to conform. It could also be internal pressures brought on by self-doubt or timidity. Pressure is not from God. He may pursue you, but He never pushes. He gave you free will and the mind of Christ. What is Jesus saying to you about your outside and inside pressures?

Lord, with all this swirling confusion in my world, I hesitate to make a move. Speak to me through Your Word in my daily reading. Take off the lid, and reduce this pressure. Show me the hidden things beyond the apparent. Reveal Your wisdom so I can move forward. Transform my thinking with Your presence. Not my will but Yours.

**Today my mind will be renewed
with God's thoughts.**

Imagine with Me

No eye has seen, no ear has heard,
and no mind has imagined what God has
prepared for those who love him.
1 Corinthians 2:9, NLT

It doesn't matter what age you are; you have a unique and creative talent to see something that isn't and think, *How can I build it?* Insight and invention are God-given qualities. His sons and daughters are problem-solvers. You're the one who thinks, *What if?* and *How can I do this?* Out of His love for you, He created you with this power of imagination. Take a no-holds-barred attitude. Be free of restrictions. Imagine with Him.

Remember that idea I had a while back, Lord? Was that You, or was it me? It keeps coming back, so it must be You. Let's take some time together today and pencil it out. I'm setting aside my time and have a pad ready to go. Meet with me, and pour Your ideas into me. Take me beyond my limitations.

Today I will imagine limitless possibilities with God.

Awaken Me

APRIL 21

The Sovereign LORD has given me his words of wisdom,
so that I know how to comfort the weary. Morning by morning he
wakens me and opens my understanding to his will.
Isaiah 50:4, NLT

The reality is this: You're not in this world just for yourself. You're here not only for God but for others. The deposits God has placed in you are deep inside. Those gifts need a little coaxing and your willingness to let it all out. Some of us are morning people, and some are night owls. He knows your schedule. However He's wired you, the Lord wants to pour something special into you so you can pour out to others.

Meet with me, Lord, in my quiet time. Speak to me about Your plans for my day. Is there someone I need to call? Who would You like me to pray for today? How can I partner with You for someone who needs comfort? Use me, Lord, to share Your love and wisdom.

Today I will awaken with God-inspired ideas.

Persistence

Don't you know that God, the true judge, will grant justice
to all his chosen ones who cry out to him night and day?
He will pour out his Spirit upon them. He will not delay
to answer you and give you what you ask for.
Luke 18:7, TPT

Jesus's Parable of the Persistent Widow is a powerful reminder to have faith and hope, stay in prayer, and not give up. The parable portrays her judge as ungodly, with no fear of God or man. And yet, the widow kept bringing her demand for justice. Her persistence paid off. So will yours. The Lord will honor your perseverance.

Isaiah 33:22 says that the Lord is our judge, lawgiver, and king.
That means You are the government of my life and circumstances.
Today, I bring some issues that need resolution to fully serve You
with what's in my heart. Help me make decisions according to Your
will. I yield my thoughts and plans and will abide by Your decision.

Today I will persist in making my requests known.

Heart and Soul

Put your heart and soul into every activity you do,
as though you are doing it for the Lord himself
and not merely for others.
Colossians 3:23, TPT

At least once in our lives, we had to do something we really didn't want to do. Everything in us wanted to go one way, but circumstances led us in another direction. If we're honest, it was probably more than once. The key to successfully making it through was your heart attitude. Maybe you're still in that situation. Trust the Lord that this trial is still under His watch. He's for you. Do whatever that hard thing is for Him with your whole heart and soul.

Everything in me cries out for release from this situation. But, God, I know You are for me, and You've got my back. This assignment may even be heaven-ordered. I want to be honest with You. I don't like it. I don't enjoy it. So, please change my heart attitude. Accept this as a sacrifice of praise, and give me Your grace to give it my all.

Today I will give the Lord my best.

For You Always

Who then is the one who condemns? No one. Christ Jesus
who died—more than that, who was raised to life—is at
the right hand of God and is also interceding for us.
Romans 8:34, NIV

It's not unusual to think that we're alone in our situations. We all tend to think no one really understands. That may be true in the natural, but it certainly is not true in the spiritual. Your champion consistently prays for your success. If Jesus was willing to give His life for you, wouldn't He also want to see you experience life to its fullest? Of course He wants that for you!

Oh Lord Jesus, having You in my life is everything. I can
confidently approach the throne of grace through Your name and
precious blood. I am never alone when I need Your help. You are
the Prince of Peace and have the words of life. Appeal to the
Father for my situation, and send angelic help. My victory is in
Your victory. Battle for me, Jesus.

Today I will praise Jesus as my intercessor.

Empowered

APRIL 25

You empower me for victory with your wraparound
presence. Your power within makes me strong to subdue.
By stooping down in gentleness, you made me great!
Psalm 18:35, TPT

As we go a little deeper into His calling on our lives, it's imperative that we recognize it's not us. It's Jesus alive in us with the presence of Holy Spirit. Whatever has been circling in your thoughts, pressing through in you day after day, is a God-thought that needs some attention. We often hear, "Where God guides, God provides." Trust that unction. It's the power of Holy Spirit to do the impossible through you.

Lord, it seems like every time I stop, look, and listen, I'm impressed
with something beyond my wildest notion. Is that You? It must be.
You're calling me to take a risk and follow Your lead. I recognize
my weakness, but I'm ready and willing to take it up and run with
Your power. I want my life to bring You glory. I accept Your
challenge.

Today I will be empowered by God's call.

Trailblazer

APRIL 26

We look away from the natural realm and we focus our attention and expectation *onto Jesus who birthed faith within us and who leads us forward into faith's perfection.*
Hebrews 12:2, TPT

Whether we're stay-at-home moms, workers, entrepreneurs, or retired, there is a spark in us that never goes out. There's a pull that longs for more—more of Him, more of us, more of life. When you give in to that longing, possibilities open wide. Faith in that vision calls you forward to more. You become a pioneer of faith and a trailblazer for the Spirit of truth. Like Abraham, Joshua, Deborah, or John the Baptist, it's time for you to leave the wilderness behind and step into your assignment.

I hear You loud and clear, Lord. I'm ready to shake off doubt and unbelief. You really are calling me up and out. I agree with You. Nothing is impossible for You. You've commissioned me for the impossible, and my heart agrees and says yes! Now, let my faith answer Your truth. Make it so, Lord.

Today I will blaze a new trail by faith.

Zigzag or Ziklag?

So David inquired of the LORD, saying,
"Shall I pursue this troop? Shall I overtake them?"
And He answered him, "Pursue, for you shall surely
overtake them *and without fail recover* all.*"*
1 Samuel 30:8, NKJV

The Word contains testimonies of heroes who conquered significant challenges. David's men were about to stone him over their loss of family and possessions, but he *"encouraged himself in the Lord"* (1 Samuel 30:6). Then he did the next best thing: he asked the Lord what to do. His actions are an example for us. The Lord is for you, especially when He's given you an assignment. Strengthen your faith through worship first and foremost.

There is no one like You, Lord. I honor Your supremacy in all things that matter to me. When I'm down and seem to be zigging when I should be zagging, You are always present to put me back on track. You renew my spirit and clear my thoughts when I praise You. Thank You for being my victory.

Today I will inquire of the Lord
and hear His answer.

Peace and Quiet

APRIL 28

*And the effect of righteousness will be peace, and the result
of righteousness, quietness and trust forever.*
Isaiah 32:17, ESV

One of the benefits of spring cleaning is the satisfaction you feel
when you survey your progress. You've made room for more.
Aligning yourself with what God has said and is saying about you is
like clearing away the layers to get to the core of you. Holy Spirit
engages you to know more about what Jesus has done for you. Once
you understand His righteousness is in you and upon you, peace,
quietness, and trust are yours—forever.

*I'm beginning to get it, Lord. I've enjoyed our quiet encounters.
This month has been a time of clearing out all of the extraneous to
make room for more of You in my life. I'm beginning to experience
a new outlook on my life and how to be more effective. I trust You
with this transition, and You can trust me to continue to make
progress.*

**Today I will experience His peace while
I enjoy our quiet time.**

Wellspring of Love

APRIL 29

Above all else, guard your heart,
for everything you do flows from it.
Proverbs 4:23, NIV

Let's be honest. One of our most difficult challenges in life is guarding our hearts from offense, hurt, rejection, disappointment, and bitterness. Don't put it past the enemy to shoot a good one at you through the mouth of a loved or respected one. Here's the kicker: he's a liar. You've learned the power of your eternal relationship these past months. You are loved, treasured, and equipped to accomplish whatever He's placed in your heart. So guard it.

Thank You, Lord, for expanding my heart. You have reassured me of Your forgiveness. You have encouraged me by highlighting my gifts. Best of all, You have empowered me to pursue that God-sized dream I now dream. My heart is Yours. You've covered it with the precious blood of Jesus, sealed it with Holy Spirit's infilling, and expanded it with the Father's favor. How could I not guard these extraordinary gifts of love?

Today I will guard the life of God's
love in my heart.

Marvelous You

APRIL 30

This was the LORD's doing;
It is marvelous in our eyes.
Psalm 118:23, NKJV

Aren't you filled with wonder over your progress so far? You've unlocked treasures of truth in the Word of God. You've prayed heartfelt prayers and made daily affirmations declaring His truth about you. As young children, we wanted to see, smell, touch, and experience everything. No longer constrained by your world or circumstance, you can take that childlike, mature faith into the next phase of discovering the *me* you were meant to be. You've cleaned out the old and are ready for the new you.

What a journey this spring has been, Lord. Now that I've come this far, I look forward to where You are taking me in the months ahead. My challenges may not have changed much, but my attitude toward them certainly has. I am grateful for Your constant companionship. The revelation of Your love and delight in me just as I am lifts my spirit and keeps me looking to what's ahead.

Today I will praise the Lord for
His marvelous work in my life.

May

AM I BLOOMING
WHERE I'M PLANTED?

Spring is on full display in May. The air is fresher, birds are chirping, and we're alive with promise. Our senses are attuned to pleasant fragrances and beauty all around us. It's a perfect time for long walks and talks with the Lord. You've assessed your strengths and weaknesses, evaluated your relationships, and made a few course corrections. There's a new rhythm and flow since you've heard the heart of God for yourselves and others.

As the weeks progress this month, you will explore a fresh outlook of the *me* that the Father uniquely designed inside you. You'll begin by celebrating the new you and sharing your growth with the world around you. At mid-month, you'll embark on the challenge of engaging your faith and gifts. You'll complete your month's journey as you stop and smell the roses with the Lord.

No Maydays Allowed

MAY 1

And let us not grow weary while doing good,
for in due season we shall reap if we do not lose heart.
Galatians 6:9, NKJV

"Mayday! Mayday!" is a distress call based on a French phrase meaning "help me." With your renewed identity and assurance of eternal, personal, and immediate aid, distress is no longer in your vocabulary. For you, it's different. You're just starting to uncover all the *me* God created you to be. So, keep growing! Your heart is strong, your faith encouraged, and your attitude of gratitude anchors you to the Lord and lifts your spirit. Your due season is ahead.

It's a beautiful day, Lord, and I have You to thank for that. Thank You for reviving my outlook and plans for today and this month. I am anticipating great fruit in my life, and I have You to thank for it. I am not weary and no longer come to You in distress or desperation. My joy is talking and walking with You in peace daily.

Today I will reap peace, joy, and energy.

Get Up and Go

MAY 2

The power of the Lord came on Elijah and,
tucking his cloak into his belt, he ran ahead
of Ahab all the way to Jezreel.
1 Kings 18:46, NIV

There's a story here that should encourage you. The prophet Elijah heard the sound of rain in his spirit before he saw it. He bent to the ground, buried his face, and prayed. As he continued to pray, Elijah sent his servant seven times to see if the rain had come. When the servant reported a cloud the size of a man's hand, Elijah began to run. The power of the Lord came upon him for extraordinary speed. What has the Lord spoken to your spirit these months? Are you ready to run?

Lord, You've put something in my heart that only You could do. I'm
unsure if I have the gifts or talents to act on Your thoughts, but I am
willing. Like Elijah, I am ready to bend my will to Yours. Help me
now to pray with faith for all that is needed.

Today I will get up my courage and go with God's flow.

First Steps

MAY 3

Let the wise hear and increase in learning,
and the one who understands obtain guidance.
Proverbs 1:5, ESV

When we first move on a new path, we often feel nervous. There are mixed emotions of excitement, fear, anticipation, and even exhilaration. In times like these, a special someone gives you the encouragement and steady hand you desperately need. Toddlers need another's guidance when they begin to walk, and so do you. If you need wisdom for your first steps, ask for it. The Lord longs to lend you a hand.

Lord, I need Your favor today. I know I've got You every day in every way, but I need more education and resources. I've committed to stepping out in a new direction, but I'm a bit shaky. Will You watch over my shoulder as I search for help? Many have gone before me. I want to grow from their experience and build from there. I don't want to fall, but I promise to get back up and try again if I do.

Today I will take my first steps toward
walking out the new me.

Untangle Me

MAY 4

Therefore if the Son makes you free,
you shall be free indeed.
John 8:36, NKJV

Imagine a tangled water hose. The water might slowly drip, but after we deal with the twist, it gushes out. That's what this journey to uncover the real *me* is all about. Every son or daughter who receives salvation also discovers unique gifts from Holy Spirit. Your delight is discovering those deposits and letting them flow. Your spiritual life can be like a kinked water hose. Let Him work out the tangle with His wisdom guiding you through the process. What a gusher you will produce!

This is such an exciting time, Lord. I'm beginning to feel a new freedom of expression. Your love is pouring in, washing away all the doubt and unbelief that have clogged me. I know it's You, Jesus, and I am so grateful. It's like You're taking me to a new place of possibility. I want to grow even more, Holy Spirit. Guide me as I uncover who You and Your gifts are in me.

Today I will think, Unkink, throughout my day.

I Am Known

But whoever loves God is known by God.
1 Corinthians 8:3, NIV

When we were children, we played games where we had to have a secret password to get into the clubhouse. In the kingdom of heaven, the password is L-O-V-E. You know you are accepted, loved, and belong solely to the Lord. No adversary, circumstance, or outside influence can take that away from you. You are known and loved. Period. The love of the Father calls you to His eternal purpose, and your love for Him wants to fulfill that purpose.

Father, You so loved me that You sent Your Son to die for me. If I were the only one in the world, You would still send Jesus just for me, and He would still go to the cross just for me. I know it from my head to my toes and from my mind to my heart. Your password isn't a secret at all. It is L-O-V-E! Everyone should know Your password. It's free, protected, and shareable.

Today I will celebrate that I am known and loved.

I Am His Gift

A spiritual gift is given to each of us
so we can help each other.
1 Corinthians 12:7, NLT

We think of talent as singing, painting, baking, gardening, sports, adding numbers, and solving mysteries. That's what the natural world thinks. In the life of the believer, there's so much more. Holy Spirit motivates your spirit to use your God-given talents for others. He will inspire you to express His love in various ways. Usually, it's an impression that comes out of nowhere. When you feel that urge, follow it and give back to the giver.

Holy Spirit, I want You to know something. I'm beginning to think there's much more of You inside of me than I'm giving out. I don't want to be timid anymore. I want to live my love for You out loud. You can jump-start me on a new adventure. I'm willing to risk it, especially if You are behind it. Can You speak a little louder so I can be sure it's You?

Today I will look for ways to give to others.

A Can-Do Attitude

MAY 7

I have strength for *all things in the* One *strengthening me.*
Philippians 4:13, BLB

That first step is challenging, like jumping off a high dive or riding a roller-coaster. But what a thrill it is after you do it! What is fear anyway? To most of us, it's a shaky feeling in the pit of our stomachs when we risk our bodies or reputations when facing a challenge. A victorious life means that if Christ has called you to do something, He's infused you with *His* strength and confidence. Remember, you're a team, and He says you can do this.

Lord, I hear Philippians 4:13, which says, "I can do all things through Christ who strengthens me." It sounds like someone building themselves up to do something they don't really think they can do. So, Lord, let's get this straight. If You put something hard to do in my heart, You promise to change my thinking and strengthen me to finish the job well. If You say so, then I do too.

Today, Jesus, *we* will do this together.

Sharing Is Caring

MAY 8

And do not neglect doing good and sharing,
for with such sacrifices God is pleased.
Hebrews 13:16, NASB

We were encouraged to share our toys or a turn on the swing as children. Today, as Christians, we are encouraged to give our time, energy, and lives to the one who saved us, set us free, and called us to love others more than ourselves. If we're honest, we sometimes think, *What about* me? That's the point. Believe it, this *is* your time. That's the beauty of His rich blessing: receiving, giving, and sharing. What goes around will come around. Even if it doesn't, God is pleased with you.

Oh God! I am so grateful for what You're doing in my heart. You see everything I do for those around me. I don't do it for the praise of men. I do it for You. Thank You for changing my focus and attitude. You've taken such weight off my shoulders, and it's easier to breathe. Thank You for freeing me.

Today I am pleasing God when I give
myself freely to others.

Branch Out

Wickedness never brings stability,
but the godly have deep roots.
Proverbs 12:3, NLT

Jesus is our firm foundation, the cornerstone of everything we build our lives on. When there is a threat to your livelihood or the security of your home, you know whom you can trust and turn to. Through experience, you are now deeply rooted and grounded in your faith. The Lord has shown Himself true and faithful to you. You are learning to stand firm and persevere with His help. You are now ready to branch out into a new level of authority from this position.

Lord, I'm hearing Your call for strength and confidence in the authority You have given me over my life and the issues that impact it. I see what is true and false, good and bad, evil and righteous. Increase in me to have a faith-filled impact on my family, friends, coworkers, and others. Let the world around me see the real me You're forging for battle.

Today I will branch out of my comfort zone.

Live Generously

Give generously to them and do so without a grudging heart;
then because of this the LORD your God will bless you in all your
work and in everything you put your hand to.
Deuteronomy 15:10, NIV

How many of us have spent so many years doing for others that we begin to feel unappreciated? You may not complain out loud, but you're thinking about it inside. Busted! Our culture, how we grew up with "The Golden Rule," shapes our attitudes and actions. The truth is that those who experience the generous love of God express it generously and thus fulfill the circle of love. God sees every kindness and sacrifice you make.

Lord, there are days when I don't know if I've got enough juice for others. In times like these, I can't express how grateful I am that You provide the stamina and the resources to do what You're asking me to do. We've become a great team. No one likes a complainer, and that includes me. So keep me cheerful, supplied, generous, and focused on You and You alone.

Today I will live generously.

Mendable

My dearest brothers and sisters, take this to heart:
Be quick to listen, but slow to speak.
And be slow to become angry.
James 1:19, TPT

It's interesting that mendable rhymes with bendable. Part of your growth journey is discovering and unveiling the real *me* in your relationship with God and others. As you bend under His loving guidance, it mends the hurts, the abandoned feelings, and even your hidden fears. From that revelation, you'll find you treat others with the same compassion you have received. You are learning to love one another as He loved you.

Lord, I am amazed at how much You are changing me! I used to be so ready to complain or grumble under my breath. Thank You for accepting me just as I am but then remaking me into Your image. I feel so much better about myself. And to top it all off, I feel so much better about the people around me.

Today I will rejoice about bendable, mendable me.

The Narrow Beam

Before you do anything, put your trust totally
in God and not in yourself.
Then every plan you make will succeed.
Proverbs 16:3, TPT

Think of a balance beam. The margins are narrow, and once you've climbed up, you must be ready to make adjustments. What's the one caution you have? Keep your eyes focused on the goal. Don't look down, and don't look back. You may wobble a bit, but you'll get there. That's what your walk with the Lord is like. Stay on the beam with the eyes of your heart focused, and trust in Him.

Sometimes, Lord, I feel a little queasy about what's ahead of me. I know You have a destiny for me. I'm just a little hesitant about getting there. On my own, I don't think I can do it. But I am strengthening myself with Your promises. When I lose my balance, give me Your steadying hand. I trust You. I will follow You. I will stay with You. And I will give You all the glory when we get there together.

Today I will stay balanced and focused on the Lord.

His Grace Alone

But he said to me, "My grace is sufficient for you, for my power is made perfect in weakness." Therefore I will boast all the more gladly about my weaknesses, so that Christ's power may rest on me.
2 Corinthians 12:9, NIV

Our problem isn't, "I won't." Our problem is, "I don't *think* I can." Every son and daughter of the Lord Almighty wants to please Him with their obedience. But if you're honest, behind every assignment lurks that stabbing doubt or twinge of unbelief that you must fight off. You might as well face it. If the Lord asks you to do something, He fully expects you to do it, but *with* His help. That's called grace, and it's always abundant for the willing.

Your Word is so rich, Lord. I don't know what I would do without the encouragement of reading what others, like Paul, had to deal with and still accomplish Your assigned tasks. Sometimes, I face molehills. Other times, I face mountains. But I can always count on Your grace and willingness to empower me.

Today I will continually praise the Lord for His grace.

Share the Joy

Come, everyone! Clap your hands!
Shout to God with joyful praise!
Psalm 47:1, NLT

Ever notice how it's hard to keep your excitement inside when you've conquered a challenge? You just want to share it. That's what overcoming fear and stepping out in faith will do for you. Suddenly, you find an inner strength that wasn't there before. It oozes from your pores and affects everyone around you. When you fully discover the *me* you were created to be, you can't help but share your joy with those around you.

Lord, I am amazed at what I've begun to feel inside. You are transforming my hold-it-back attitude into a let's-go attitude, and it's beautiful. There's a new freedom in me that only You could ignite. And, Lord, I don't want this just for myself. Give me insight, Holy Spirit, in ways I can help others with my testimony of Your grace and what You've done for me. Give me opportunities wherever I go.

Today I will encourage others with
the Lord's progress in me.

He Will Do It

"The LORD did it!" David exclaimed.
"He burst through my enemies like a raging flood!"
So he named that place Baal-perazim (which means
"the Lord who bursts through").
2 Samuel 5:20, NLT

Every one of us has an area that needs a breakthrough. We're human! Some need healing, some need reconciliation, and some have seemingly insurmountable barriers. Maybe you need favor, a jolt, a revelation, or a key. Whatever it is, the Lord is on your side. He is the Lord of breakthroughs. The Lord is your very present help and will always lead you to victory.

I get so excited when I set my mind and heart on the other side of my need. Lord, I have seen You break through circumstances for me in the past, so my faith is stirred up and encouraged to see how You will answer this time. Some struggles are known only to You, but others are known to others. I want You to get the glory, Lord. Show Yourself strong on my behalf. I'd love a testimony in this test.

Today I am excited for the breakthrough.

Discernment

The wise in heart are called discerning,
and gracious words promote instruction.
Proverbs 16:21, NIV

One of the greatest gifts that comes with age is discernment. We're learning to be prudent and mature in our daily lives. Experience, doing a job of any kind, has its instruction. Learning from your mistakes is a great teacher as well. However, nothing compares to our sensitivity to the presence of Holy Spirit. He has a delightful way of helping you to focus on what is real, true, and right. Then, you get to share it with others.

Holy Spirit, so many people count on me to have the right answer. Growing with You over the years has been a marvelous experience. Thank You for helping me understand Your Word as I read. It's like You're speaking about something very pertinent to my day. It surprises me how often verses I read come up in my daily conversations with others. Discernment is an incredible gift, especially in today's world of confusion.

Today I will practice discernment
when I'm with others.

Putting on My Spurs

MAY 17

*And let us consider how we may spur one another
on toward love and good deeds.*
Hebrews 10:24, NIV

Every spiritual warrior understands the importance of putting on your armor every day. The apostle Paul told us to put on the belt of truth, the breastplate of righteousness, the gospel of peace boots, the shield of faith, and pick up the sword of the Spirit (the Word of God). It's how we're clothed with protection and power in prayer for ourselves and others. Metal spurs are attached to boots and are used to encourage horses to giddy up. It's time to strap on your spurs and kick it up a notch.

Lord, putting on my armor is easy when I'm in a battle. Forgive me for neglecting to put it on every day. I recognize that You designed it for a daily purpose. Help me to remember to dress in my gear each morning. That way, I'll have a ready answer for myself or a friend in need.

Today I will dress in my armor and add my spurs.

Leap to It

MAY 18

For by You I can run against a troop,
By my God I can leap over a wall.
Psalm 18:29, NKJV

We look before we leap, leap to avoid danger, and leap in the dark. But we also leap at a chance, take a leap of faith, and leap for joy. All of these take courage and a willingness to move. As you partner with God, you will discover an added synergy. It's like a booster rocket that kicks in. Faith does that for you, especially when the unction to do something challenging comes from the Lord.

Lord, You've been bringing something to my attention off and on for quite some time. If this is really Your idea, then I'm ready, willing, and just about able to do it. Frankly, I need Your Holy Spirit's power and wisdom to get me off the ground. Guide me in my thinking and prayer time. I might be a bit cautious, but I'm ready to leap with You.

Today I will take Your hand and leap with You.

Tested Trust

But when I am afraid, I will put my trust in you.
I praise God for what he has promised.
I trust in God, so why should I be afraid?
What can mere mortals do to me?
Psalm 56:3–4, NLT

There comes a time in everyone's life when we finally *do* take that leap of faith. Building confidence takes time, but no person or situation can hold you back once you have established a sure foundation. It's the little tests and trials where you've seen God come through for you that become the launching pad for greater faith in action. Take some time today to recount the times He's pulled through for you.

> *There's nothing quite like the peace I feel when I'm in Your presence, Lord. I love bringing my problems to You and sorting them out one by one. You know the end from the beginning of each of these issues. Thank You for being in the middle with me. Your wisdom brings me comfort, as well as ingenious ideas toward resolution. There's none like You!*

Today I will again put my trust in the Lord.

Closer than a Brother

MAY 20

And the LORD, He is the One who goes before you.
He will be with you, He will not leave you
nor forsake you; do not fear nor be dismayed.
Deuteronomy 31:8, NKJV

It's just a fact of life that sometimes our families, friends, or people we look up to will fail us. But, as the saying goes, "No man is an island." Both faith and failure have ripple effects. You get to choose which side of the island you're pitching your tent. Your great comforter, as well as your motivator, is the promise of your Savior that He would send His Spirit to be with you always.

Lord, there are some days when I find myself in a hard and lonely place. What would I do without You? You are so faithful to me. I can put on some worship music, open my Bible to my favorite Scriptures, or call a spiritual mom or dad to pray with me. Thank You for keeping Your promise to be close.

Today I will sense the Lord's nearness.

Write the Vision

MAY 21

Write the vision And make it *plain on tablets,*
That he may run who reads it.
Habakkuk 2:2, NKJV

We're almost at the midpoint in this devotional. Take a moment today and read Habakkuk. It's only three chapters but has insight into our days and seasons. You see what's going on around you and in your life. You've stood your watch and need to hear from the Lord. Grab a yellow pad or journal and pen. What is the Lord saying to you today? What's His vision for you and through you?

Lord, spring is in full bloom, and the heat of summer is around the corner. Thank You for being with me through this journey these past few months. We've come a long way, but I still have a long way to go. What's on Your heart for me today, Lord? I will list a few things and invite You to share Your thoughts with me. Who is the me *You see? Help me write the vision.*

Today I will write the vision the Lord gives me.

Yoked to Jesus

MAY 22

Come to me, all you who are weary and burdened,
and I will give you rest. Take my yoke upon you and learn
from me, for I am gentle and humble in heart,
and you will find rest for your souls.
Matthew 11:28–29, NIV

There are days when we realize we are shouldering way too much. It's normal to want to do your fair share and even go beyond your limit when needed. That's the beauty of a caring heart. Jesus loves that about you. But don't lose sight of caring for yourself when you've depleted your resources. You are more important than what you do! He wants to share your burden.

Oh Jesus, Your words are comforting. You know how to reach my mind and emotions at the right time and in my greatest need. I am so grateful that I can run to You and share the deepest things in my heart. We will plow this field of troubles together. I am yoked to You forever!

Today I will take Jesus's yoke and learn from Him.

Mustard Seed Faith

If you have faith as small as a mustard seed,
you can say to this mulberry tree, "Be uprooted
and planted in the sea," and it will obey you.
Luke 17:6, NIV

Have you ever thought about the size of a mustard seed? It's about one to two millimeters or barely over the sixteenth mark on a one-inch ruler. You can hardly pinch it between your fingers. When God plants an idea in you, it may start small. But when Holy Spirit blows His fire, wind, and rain on it, expect it to flourish. He's planted you in good soil and will nourish you.

You are the creator of the universe! You spoke, and light was.
Everything we see, feel, touch, and smell was created by You.
Magnificent! And now, You've planted this little mustard seed idea
in my heart. I'm shaky thinking about it. But I do believe it's You.
So, if that's so, You have the power to make it grow, blossom, and
bear fruit. I commit my willingness to birth this with You.

Today I will pray that my mustard seed faith grows.

Renew

MAY 24

He saved us, not by the righteous deeds we had done,
but according to His mercy, through the washing
of new birth and renewal by the Holy Spirit.
Titus 3:5, BSB

In our Christian walks, we hear much about revive, restore, repair, regain, rejuvenate, repent, and renew. Ever thought about the word combination? "Re" means to do it again, put something back in the right order, or find something that was lost.[1] Invite the morning light of the Lord, and let Him and His Word make all things new. Spend some quiet time with the Lord, and let Him renew you.

My spirit rejoices in You, Lord. I am so grateful for what You've done for me and in me. You redeem everything about me. You give me purpose for my days, peace for my nights, and possibilities for my tomorrows. Thank You for Your mercy. You and I know I'm not perfect, but You are in all Your ways, Holy Spirit, and I trust You to lead and guide me. Keep me new in You every day.

Today I will be renewed in my spirit
with Holy Spirit's help.

A Pregnant Pause

MAY 25

He supplies life and breath and all things
to every living being.
Acts 17:25, TPT

Sometimes, we just have to stop and smell the roses, even in our God conversations. Some call it a pregnant pause. It's when you take in life-giving air and expel the stress, the rush, the worry, the whatever is pressing on your peace. A walk in the garden, twenty minutes on the couch, or maybe just sitting in the parking lot will do the trick. We all need God-orchestrated CPR sometimes so that new life can be birthed. How do you like to pause with God?

Holy Spirit, You are the breath of life. You are *life. Today, I need a little re-lifing. Meet me in this quiet place. As I breathe out my troubles and concerns, take them far from me. I place them at the feet of Jesus. I know You both are interceding for me before the Father's throne. I am so grateful. Here I am. I am quiet. I am listening. I am waiting.*

Today I will pause, exhale my worries,
and breathe in new life.

I Am Listening

MAY 26

The LORD came and stood there, calling as at
the other times, "Samuel! Samuel!" Then Samuel said,
"Speak, for your servant is listening."
1 Samuel 3:10, NIV

We can lose sight of the obvious when our responsibilities are so great. We set our own goals, and the driver in us pushes hard. The realist knows that slow and steady wins the race. What if the Lord came to you, stood there, and called you? But you didn't answer. Would He come again? What if you were with the 120 followers of Jesus in the upper room after His ascension but left on the ninth day? Wait. Don't give up.

Lord, make my ears sensitive to Your voice. Help me recognize Your tone, timbre, whisper, and shout. Jesus, You said that Your sheep know Your voice. Help me to hear Your voice when You speak through others. Give me the discernment to know when You are calling and to respond immediately. I am Your handmaiden. Speak to me now.

Today I will listen with both ears for the Lord.

Innocence Reborn

MAY 27

Truly I say to you, unless you change and become like children, you will not enter the kingdom of heaven.
Matthew 18:3, NASB

Humility is not an easy virtue to acquire. It goes against every grain of your individuality. From your very first steps, it's all about independence and going it on your own. Jesus teaches us that His kingdom is for the young at heart who know their God, serve their God, and depend on Him. As you continue rediscovering the *me* He created you to be, rekindle the innocence of childlike faith.

Lord, life has its way of pushing and pulling me in all sorts of directions. I need Your help with important decisions and a game plan for this adult life I'm supposed to lead. I am so grateful that I can come to You as Your child. I trust Your counsel and guidance. A lot of people count on me to be wise and strong. I trust You for that and more.

Today I will rest with Jesus and be restored.

A Matter of Perspective

He has made everything beautiful in its time.
He has also set eternity in the human heart; yet no one
can fathom what God has done from beginning to end.
Ecclesiastes 3:11, NIV

What is time? To us, it's days, weeks, months, years, and decades. To God, it isn't linear. It's circular. He sees the end from the beginning. The beginning, end, and in-between are always beautiful and filled with eternal promise and purpose to Him and for you. We often hear phrases like perfect timing, right on time, or in the nick of time. An eternal perspective in your day-to-day changes everything when it's *His* time.

Dear Lord, this day belongs to you. My space is Your space. My time is Your time. Fill it with Your presence. Give me a glimpse of Your eternal perspective on my life and destiny. Surely, You have plans for me I have yet to discover. I long to partner with You. You've planted eternity in my heart. I am Yours, and You are mine.

Today I will see my life from God's perspective.

Pressing On

MAY 29

*I press on toward the goal for the prize of
the upward call of God in Christ Jesus.*
Philippians 3:14, NASB

There's no more sitting back and waiting for your destiny to catch up. It's time to get in God's flow, answer the upward call, and put your shoulders to the wheel. Notice that Paul said *in* Christ Jesus. Once you're *in* Christ, you have His authority and anointing to do what the Father has written in your Book of Destiny.[1] The word "press" means to positively pursue with all haste.[2] It's time to roll.

I finally hear You, Lord. You have divinely inspired plans for my life. Thank You for changing my attitude and perspective. It's no more, Woe is me. It's more like, Oh boy, I get to do this with Jesus! I am excited about what my future holds. I trust Holy Spirit's guidance and direction. You already had my ears and my heart. Now, You have my energy and commitment.

**Today I will press on and upward
to God's call on my life.**

Wise Words

Incline your ear, and hear the words of the wise,
and apply your heart to My knowledge,
for it will be pleasant if you keep them within you,
if all of them are ready on your lips.
Proverbs 22:17–18, ESV

We never, ever have to go it alone. When you accepted Jesus Christ as your Savior, you got the wisest best friend ever as your bonus. You have the eternal words of Jesus, but you gained wisdom, knowledge, and understanding through Holy Spirit's revelation. He is constantly whispering to you, "This way. See that. Hear this. Do that." Jesus had the Father's direction. You have Holy Spirit.

Holy Spirit, this is an exciting time to listen and learn from You. I love it when I know in my knower that You've given me a revelation. I love mysteries and hidden things. You make learning more about You, Jesus, and the Father so fulfilling. And best of all, when I speak Your words in a declaration, I know angels engage in battle for me and those I pray for.

Today I will be pleasantly surprised by Holy Spirit.

In Full Bloom

MAY 31

The LORD will guide you continually, giving you water
when you are dry and restoring your strength.
You will be like a well-watered garden, like an ever-flowing spring.
Isaiah 58:11, NLT

When the Lord restores vision and purpose, renewed strength and vigor bubble up from the inside. It may start slowly, but you eventually flow confidently with the Lord's guidance. That's when your transformation inside splashes on the world outside of you. You can't contain your joy. In fact, joy is a feeling that must have an outlet. You're in full bloom now.

What a month it's been, Lord. You've been here every step of the way, guiding me out of the dumps, lifting my spirit, and shining Your light on multiple areas. You have restored my strength. But, most importantly, You've revived my vision for what is possible in my tomorrows. There is a new power I'm sensing in my rest. It's hard to explain, Lord. Thank You for awakening me.

Today I will enjoy blooming fully for the Lord.

June

AM I READY FOR THE NEXT LEVEL?

In June, hard-working students reap the rewards of their educational journey. Family and friends cheer them on as they receive their diplomas and graduate to a new challenge in life. Family and friends also beam with delight as they watch their June bride walk down the aisle. We smile dotingly over her beautiful white dress and veiled face as she embarks on her covenant journey with the man of her dreams. In both cases, we are the participants and the witnesses.

You've spent almost half a year growing and activating your faith in a new way by rediscovering the Father's unique design for you as an individual. You're now ready to move past secure foundational truths and elementary prayers. It's time for promotion from *me* to *we*. This month's focus will address expansion in all areas of your personal life as you become the *me* the Father created you to be for *them*.

Always a Student

JUNE 1

Get all the advice and instruction you can,
so you will be wise the rest of your life.
Proverbs 19:20, NLT

One of the greatest gifts the Father has given us is the ability to learn and increase in knowledge. By acquiring it, we gain wisdom that comes with age and experience. Have you ever wondered why? Yes, you could improve your technical skills for work and career or become proficient at an activity you enjoy. But is there something more? God wants you to impact the world and pass it on to the next generation. How will you do that?

Father, thank You for giving me a willing heart and a bright mind. I am in awe of the wonders You've created in my world. You've given me a curious nature that wants to know more. I know I've reached a certain age where school books aren't necessary. But, Lord, I never want to be so sure of myself that I can't learn a thing or two, especially from You.

Today the Lord will teach me something new
to share with others.

Me, Myself, and Them

JUNE 2

*Restore to me the joy of your salvation and grant
me a willing spirit, to sustain me.*
Psalm 51:12, NIV

Everyone in our spheres of influence picks up on our moods and attitudes. The vibes you put off at home, work, and the general public are cues to your emotions. What are your unspoken messages? What do you do when you're down and out and nothing seems to work? You stir yourself up. You can go to the throne room of grace. And with a good dose of activated faith, you can ask for what you need—not just for yourself but for them as well.

Holy Spirit, I recognize that not every day is all about me. Sometimes, it's about others in my life. I'm coming to You today to fill me with Your grace, peace, and joy. I love it when You prod me to be agreeable and pleasant. Bad moods don't help any situation. I submit my swirling thoughts and grumbling to You. Restore my joy.

Today will be all about them instead of me.

Diligence Pays Off

JUNE 3

The plans of the diligent certainly lead *to advantage,*
But everyone who is in a hurry certainly comes *to poverty.*
Proverbs 21:5, NASB

There are days, maybe even seasons, when we're just done. We've put all we have into something, and there's no more juice. As a believer, you know there's another option. You start with rest. You put your feet up, close your eyes, and let your body recoup. Then you plug your spirit into Holy Spirit and recharge your batteries. It works every time. When you are diligent in seeking Him, He will never disappoint you.

Holy Spirit, I've been overloaded with all my doing for myself and others. I'm worn out and depleted. I come to You today in a posture of rest. My eyes are closed. My ears are open. My mind is calm. My heart and spirit are seeking You now. Help me to sort out all that's going on around me. Fix my focus, and show me Your plans. I'm ready for a reset.

Today I will be diligent to seek Holy Spirit's help.

God's Masterpiece

JUNE 4

For we are God's masterpiece.
He has created us anew in Christ Jesus, so we can
do the good things he planned for us long ago.
Ephesians 2:10, NLT

Have you ever considered what you look like as God's painting? Of course, the artist always enjoys His work. But *why* does He paint? We visit art galleries and museums and marvel at the interpretations of artists captured on canvas. They paint because they love to and want us to enjoy their creations. So does the Lord. Think of it this way. Father God is the artist, Jesus is the brush, and Holy Spirit is the paint. What was on His mind when He painted you?

It's too wonderful to think I am Your masterpiece, Lord. You created me to do good things from the beginning. I'm just starting to figure it out. You didn't simply paint me for You but to touch others' lives. That's humbling, but it's also exciting. I'm ready to do the good things.

Today I will think about what good things
the master has planned for me.

Eyes on You

JUNE 5

Teach me to do your will, for you are my God;
may your good Spirit lead me on level ground.
Psalm 143:10, NIV

Many have been blessed with parents, teachers, and mentors to help shape our young minds. As we mature, we are attracted to a broader selection of voices. Today, we have television, smartphones, computers, and podcasts offering a mixture of information, suggestions, and indoctrination. Remember when Mom and teachers would say, "1-2-3, eyes on me," and we'd respond, "1-2-3, eyes on you"? Today, more than ever, Holy Spirit is calling you to keep your eyes on Him and your ears open to His still, small voice.

Holy Spirit, there is so much mixture in my world right now. Even among believers, there are many different opinions. I ask You to lead me to the level path where obstacles to Your truth disappear. Keep me grounded in Your Word. Cause me to hear Your still, small voice, and help me to keep my eyes on You alone.

Today I will keep my eyes on the Lord alone.

Diamond in the Making

JUNE 6

Beloved, do not be surprised at the fiery trial when
it comes upon you to test you, as though something
strange were happening to you.
1 Peter 4:12, ESV

As we move toward destiny, we shouldn't be surprised at the
confrontations we face. It could be a personal battle or an
interpersonal one. Temptation and trials seem to come when moving
to the next level. Take heart! Your spirit is like carbon deep in the
earth. Intense heat and pressure are producing a diamond in you. Its
value comes when cut and polished, resulting in inner light and
lasting beauty. Daughter of God, you're shaping up beautifully as
you cling to God.

I shouldn't be surprised by my fiery trials, Lord. This walk with You
can be challenging sometimes. But I know You are forever on my
side and have my best interests at heart. You are forging character,
stamina, faith, trust, and many other valuable kingdom qualities.
You are the King of my heart, and I love the treasure You are
forging in me as Your bride.

Today I am not surprised by trials,
for You are always with me.

Staying Power

*If you stay in this land, I will build you up and not
tear you down; I will plant you and not uproot you.*
Jeremiah 42:10, NIV

Israel was defeated by Babylon and in captivity for seventy years.
What was the Lord's counsel? "Do your best. Stay here and count
on Me. I will be with you." One of our greatest faith gifts is trusting
the Lord's promises from His Word. You and your household might
be facing a challenge, but trust Him. The Lord is with you.

*Jesus, many are watching me in this hard season. They look up to
me, and I don't want to disappoint them or You. I sometimes feel
like that father who told You, "I believe. Help my unbelief."[1] I trust
You to give me the wisdom and staying power I need to stand firm
in my faith. I won't run from this. I will stand with You and rejoice
at the fruit You will bring forth.*

Today I will stay in faith and be fruitful.

Be a Booster

JUNE 8

May the God who gives endurance and encouragement
give you the same attitude of mind toward each other that
Christ Jesus had, so that with one mind and one voice you
may glorify the God and Father of our Lord Jesus Christ.
Romans 15:5–6, NIV

Whether it's a sports game, birthday party, or Sunday church, celebrating each other is a life-bringing event. Standing as one, cheering the team and individual, and supporting the whole is what the Lord had in mind with family and community. Just as high schools have booster clubs, churches have prayer teams. Jesus's prayer was that we would be one. How can you support and boost the Lord's team?

Thank You, Jesus, for creating such a spirit of encouragement in
my life. Knowing Your heart has opened my eyes to see others
through Yours. The Father must feel so proud when His children
gather to celebrate the church You founded. Help me always to sing
Your praises to all I meet.

Today I will be the Lord's cheerleader.

Words of Grace

JUNE 9

And never let ugly or hateful words come from your mouth,
but instead let your words become beautiful gifts that encourage
others; do this by speaking words of grace to help them.
Ephesians 4:29, TPT

Spoken words can build up or tear down. They can communicate, forgive, celebrate, or criticize. The power of words is not to be denied, especially when you've been on the receiving end. If you're truthful, you've said a few you're not too proud of. This fresh walk with the Lord sets you up with His presence and power to deliver life-giving words to those around you. What beautiful gift of grace-filled words can you give someone today?

It is such a great reminder, Lord, to watch my words. On the one hand, don't let unkindness enter into my conversations. On the other hand, I can look for opportunities to extend grace with my words. As I gain confidence, peace, and fulfillment from Your words, help me do the same for others.

Today I will watch my mouth and
speak words of grace.

Gap Standers

JUNE 10

I searched for a man among them who would build up
a wall and stand in the gap before Me for the land,
so that I would not destroy it; but I found no one.
Ezekiel 22:30, NASB

We've come to a place where we can no longer stand in the shadows. The light within you is shining brighter and brighter every day. It's time to shine that light into the world around you. These days, your prayers can impact your home, workplace, and neighborhood. Wherever you are, you carry His light and can challenge the darkness. You are the one who can build that wall of protection through the blood and name of Jesus.

Father, thank You for allowing me to come before Your throne. It's a privilege to see the needs of others and know I can stand in the gap for them through prayer. I am partnering with Holy Spirit and Your Word, along with the precious blood of Jesus and the power of His name. May my prayers move Your heart on their behalf.

Today I will build a wall of protection and
bridge the gap through prayer.

Sincerely Theirs

JUNE 11

We prove ourselves by our purity, our understanding,
our patience, our kindness, by the Holy Spirit
within us, and by our sincere love.
2 Corinthians 6:6, NLT

One of the most challenging tests of our maturity as believers is the ability to be Christlike in a lost world that seems to know how to push every button. Everything fleshly within us wants to react in judgment. But in this Spirit-led walk, you're learning to hold it in, breathe it out, and listen well to what Holy Spirit is saying. God sees your sincere efforts to walk in love, and they will see it too.

Lord, sometimes it's tough to hold my reactions back. I am so grateful for my increasing sensitivity to You and Your Spirit. The longer I'm on this walk with You, the more You're chiseling away the old me and sculpting a whole new image that looks more like You. My heart is to reflect You in all I say or do. I am sincerely Yours. Help me to be sincerely theirs.

Today I will express the fruit of Holy Spirit
through my sincere love.

No Anxiety Here

JUNE 12

*Do not be anxious about anything, but in every situation,
by prayer and petition, with thanksgiving,
present your requests to God.*
Philippians 4:6, NIV

Ever notice when others know you are a praying Christian, they bring you their problems? That's not to discount their faith or even yours. What's important here is that you take *everything* to the Lord and let Him lead the battle. One of the enemy's greatest tools is to steal your peace, and it's always with a price. Mainly yours! One of the most effective tools is to take it to the Lord in prayer, with thanksgiving that He hears you, and leave it with Him.

Bringing my prayers and petitions to You, Jesus, is a privilege. I know You are interceding for me and those I present to You. Anxiety has no place at the throne of grace. May my assurance in Your love and divine wisdom bring confidence and peace to those I pray for and with.

Today I rebuke anxiety off me and those I pray for.

An "Aha" Moment

JUNE 13

Instead, speaking the truth in love, we will grow
to become in every respect the mature body
of him who is the head, that is, Christ.
Ephesians 4:15, NIV

There comes a time when we face the truth about ourselves, the direction of our lives, and our divine purposes. Some call it an epiphany; others an eye-opener or a revelation. The Lord is calling you into a deeper relationship with Himself. And from that place of intimacy, He has secrets about you to share and assignments for you to impact the lives of others.

Lord, I know the apostle Paul is talking about the unity of the body, but this speaks to me of our union. You desire to grow me into the fullness of Your image, power, and authority. I long to hear Your truth about me and Your plans for my life. I yield my thoughts to You, Lord. Open my spiritual eyes and ears to see and hear what is ahead for me. Awaken my potential in You.

Today I will have an "aha" moment with the Lord.

Switch Your Tassel

Blessed is the one who perseveres under trial because,
having stood the test, that person will receive the crown
of life that the Lord has promised to those who love him.
James 1:12, NIV

When you receive your diploma, moving the tassel from the right side to the left is traditional to indicate successful graduation to the next level. In our walks with the Lord, there isn't an outside expression of what's grown on the inside of you. That's between you and the Lord. But the world around you will experience your transformation as you pass the tests and trials into His fullness.

It's beautiful to look back over these years, Lord, and recount how many times my faith in You has pulled me through. There have been so many trials and tests that I can't count them, but You have encouraged me in every one. Today, I admire the work You've done in me. Receive my thanksgiving as I move my tassel from right to left. I'm ready for the next challenge.

Today I have graduated to the next level.

Engaged to Him

JUNE 15

You are my private garden, my treasure, my bride,
a secluded spring, a hidden fountain.
Song of Solomon 4:12, NLT

Before you launch into your destiny of expressing the fullness of Jesus Christ, your Bridegroom, He is calling you into an intimate place with Him. It is a time of engagement to discover who He is and who you are in Him. To fully grasp the magnificence of your calling, it will take your trust in His love and tender words. Reread the Bible verse for today, but put your name in place of "you." It's the *me* He's always known you to be.

Dear Jesus, I am only beginning to fully understand Your love for me and all the Father's children. I recognize that it must start with You and me. As we meet in Your private garden, let me sense Your presence, smell Your fragrance, and hear Your voice. Draw out Your eternal deposit in me. Help me to bask and then flow in Your life-giving fountain.

Today I will meet the Lord in our private garden.

My Unveiled Face

But we all, with unveiled faces, looking as in a mirror
at the glory of the Lord, are being transformed into the same
image from glory to glory, just as from the Lord, the Spirit.
2 Corinthians 3:18, NASB

Ever notice how you pick up on someone's inflections or mannerisms the more you're with them? It's true! You finish their sentences and laugh at the same jokes. Children cock their heads like Dad or make facial expressions like Mom. That's how it is with the Lord. The more time you spend with Him and His Word, the more you begin to look like Him. The world sees Him through you.

I long to look into Your eyes, Jesus. I often wonder what I would see in them. Liquid love, regal might, compassion, unlimited power? I imagine all of these and more. But today, I realize that if I were looking into Your eyes, I would see a reflection of me. What do You see in my unveiled face?

Today I will look in the mirror and see Jesus.

Becoming One

JUNE 17

*As the Scriptures say, "A man leaves his father and mother
and is joined to his wife, and the two are united into one."
This is a great mystery, but it is an illustration
of the way Christ and the church are one.*
Ephesians 5:31–32, NLT

We commit ourselves wholly when we decide to join in marriage. There is an understood two-party obligation of faithfulness, trust, and devotion. We can also apply this Scripture to leaving our pasts to make way for our futures in Jesus. Once you make that decision, there's no turning back. When you fully embrace what covenant means to love, honor, and serve, all of His becomes all of yours.

When I committed to You, Jesus, I didn't fully comprehend the majestic power in our union. As I progress in knowing You more deeply, I realize your incredible gifts are not only for me but for those I love and minister to. I'm learning that where I go, You go. Where You lead, I follow. Together, we have endless possibilities.

Today I will ponder my oneness with Jesus.

Love Taps

JUNE 18

*But the wisdom that comes from heaven is first of all pure;
then peace-loving, considerate, submissive, full of mercy
and good fruit, impartial and sincere.*
James 3:17, NIV

Don't you love the gentle love taps of Holy Spirit? No wonder the Father sent Him as a dove at Jesus's baptism. As your walk with the Lord gets deeper and stronger, you will find that He will begin to bring you assignments. He'll put people on your heart to pray for or call. You'll have a connection with someone in a checkout line. Your daily Bible reading will prompt you to pray for someone special. These are your benefits when love taps your heart.

Lord, there is nothing more exciting than partnering with You for those who need more of You. I am so grateful for Your expansion of my heart in this way. It delights me to see others' responses when I acknowledge them with a smile, a comment, or a pleasant question about their day.

Today I will enjoy sharing Holy Spirit love taps.

No Assumptions

JUNE 19

The LORD doesn't see things the way you see them.
People judge by outward appearance,
but the LORD looks at the heart.
1 Samuel 16:7, NLT

Isn't it a relief that the Lord looks at the whole of us? He doesn't pick us apart. The Lord sees us from our immature beginnings to the mature result of our walks with Him. As you grow in grace and maturity, you, too, learn to wait, hold judgment, and give others the benefit of the doubt. You have no idea how many people are watching you as you watch them. Ask the Lord to show you their hearts.

Lord, I am so grateful that You give me grace and second chances. Your tender mercy brings peace to my soul and joy to my spirit. As I begin to fully walk in Your revelation of who I am in You, help me to extend that awareness to others. Just as Your thoughts become my thoughts, may Your words become my words when I communicate with others.

Today I will see hearts differently.

One for All

For the very glory you have given to me,
I have given them so that they will be joined together
as one and experience the same unity that we enjoy.
John 17:22, TPT

As you read this title, you probably thought of the rest of the line: "and all for one." Jesus is praying His last prayer for His disciples and us before He gives His body for the ultimate sacrifice. Glorifying the Father and bringing us into union with Him was utmost on His heart. His passion was for you to know Him fully and, from that experience, express His glory through loving others as He loves you.

Dear Jesus, my heart is so grateful for the oneness I feel when I talk to You. I sense Your nearness and compassion for the issues on my heart. When I bring others to You in prayer, I know You are listening and interceding with me before the throne. You shed Your precious blood so that we can be healed by it and the power of Your name.

Today I will be one with You as You are with me.

Stir It Up

Never be lacking in zeal, but keep your
spiritual fervor, serving the Lord. Be joyful in hope,
patient in affliction, faithful in prayer.
Romans 12:11–12, NIV

When the world begins to weigh us down, it's easy to give in to despair. We start to doubt that anything will ever change or improve. But that's not the end of the story! Attitude is everything. When you concentrate on the good things—even if they were in the past—and give thanks, your remembrance stirs up hope. And hope recasts your vision for what could be. That vision then gives you purpose in a prayer of thanksgiving for what will be.

Oh Lord, it doesn't matter if I'm up, down, or all mixed up. You have a hold on me. You know precisely where my emotions are today, but You also see my tomorrows. So, today, I will remember when what looked impossible was made possible because of You. Stir up my faith as I pray.

Today I will practice patience as I stir up my faith for tomorrow.

Numbering My Days

Teach us to number our days,
that we may gain a heart of wisdom.
Psalm 90:12, NIV

Time is a funny thing. When we're young, we feel like growing up will take forever. When we're in our twenties, we feel like life has finally begun. By the time we're over forty, we start to consider where we're at and what's ahead. Moses was eighty when called to deliver Israel and wrote this psalm. In this verse, Moses is praying that we gain wisdom by looking at our end. What do you want yours to look like?

Father, the world defines the prime of our lives one way, but I choose to have You define it for me. Wherever I am, doing whatever I'm called to do and delivering it all with the best I can is all I ask for. Help me to seek Your wisdom every day of my life from now until we meet. I don't want to miss a day without You.

Today I will consider my days and
make each one count.

At the Right Time

JUNE 23

The smallest family will become a thousand people,
and the tiniest group will become a mighty nation.
At the right time, I, the LORD, will make it happen.
Isaiah 60:22, NLT

Have you ever thought about God's timing? It certainly is a mystery. God is not limited by time in His wisdom. His omniscience knows who, what, when, where, and why. He's the master at person, place, and position. And He's got His eye on you. God is a promise-keeper. Just as Isaiah prophesied, Israel became a nation. What has He said to you? His divine clock is ticking. You can be confident that God will make it happen in His timing.

Lord, Psalm 72:14 says that I am the apple of Your eye and precious in Your sight. Thank You for revealing Your love and delight in the person I am becoming. I want to be more, do more, and live Your dream more. I trust You and Your timing in my life. Give me patient endurance and hope for the future You've destined for me.

Today I will trust the Lord for His perfect timing.

Living Words

JUNE 24

For whatever was written in earlier times was written
for our instruction, so that through perseverance and the
encouragement of the Scriptures we might have hope.
Romans 15:4, NASB

As you mature in the Lord with your walk, haven't you found that the Word of God is a lamp to your feet, an anchor for your soul, and food for your spirit? The benefits of His written Word and the messages you hear or read based on His Word feed you continually. From that source, you now have life-giving words to share with others. What do you have for them today?

There is nothing more exciting, Lord, than when I'm talking with someone and a Scripture verse pops into my mind. It's as if Your words have come alive in me, my thinking, and my daily living. Holy Spirit, thank You for leading me into greater revelation on the purpose and power of Your Word for every circumstance in life. Increase even more in my interactions with others who need this living hope.

Today I will share a life-giving word with someone.

Pay It Forward

JUNE 25

May the LORD now show you kindness and faithfulness,
and I too will show you the same favor
because you have done this.
2 Samuel 2:6, NIV

Throughout the Old and New Testaments, we read about kindness and generosity like Abraham and the three strangers, David with Jonathan's son, the Good Samaritan, and Mary anointing Jesus's feet.[1] In each case, they went beyond expectations and reaped rewards. What is the lesson? When you give, you receive abundance in return. As children, sharing was hard. But as believers, we know the benefits. When you surprise others with an act of kindness, don't be shocked when they pass it on. Make someone's day special.

I love how kind and generous You are, Lord. I smile whenever I think about Exodus 33 when Moses asked to see Your glory. You told him Your goodness will pass before him. Wow. How could I not repay Your kindness to me by my giving and sharing with others? It's a privilege to honor You this way.

Today I will find a way to pay it forward.

D.U.H.J.

All Scripture is God-breathed and is useful for teaching,
rebuking, correcting and training in righteousness,
so that the servant of God may be thoroughly
equipped for every good work.
2 Timothy 3:16–17, NIV

Driving Under His Influence. Remember taking a driver training class? The instructor always made a big deal about checking the rear-view and side mirrors and looking over your shoulder when switching lanes or reversing. Why? Because you have a blind spot. As a believer, your rear-view mirror is the Word of God, and the side mirrors are your mentors and Spirit-filled friends. Before changing direction, check your mirrors.

I love how You lead me, Lord. Your Word guides me continually as
You feed my spirit and enlarge my thinking. When I wake up, I'm
hungry to hear Your voice. I listen for Your whisper and check back
with You throughout my day. I hear Your wisdom in my friends and
mentors. I'll check in again at night when I read Your Word and
review my day with You. Thank You for revealing my blind spots.

Today I will check my mirrors and turn with You.

Preparing to Launch

JUNE 27

Prepare your work outside, And make it ready for yourself
in the field; Afterward, then, build your house.
Proverbs 24:27, NASB

We're heading into uncharted waters in the months ahead. The Lord looks at the whole of you. He cares about your physical well-being and mental and emotional states just as much as your spiritual growth. It's time for the *me* in you to expand to *we* and even *they*. It begins with stretching your faith and letting Holy Spirit flow through you. You are so crucial to your family, friends, and coworkers. Ask the Lord how you can impact their lives to a greater degree.

I love being on this journey with You, Lord. Thank You for meeting
with me each day and encouraging me with Your Scriptures and the
fruitful trails You've taken me on. I recognize my worth in Your
eyes, and my confidence in You and myself is increasing. I'm ready
now to express You to my world more significantly. Fill me with
more of You so I have an overflow for them.

Today I will prepare myself for more of God in me.

Let Down Your Nets

Now when He had finished speaking,
He said to Simon, "Put out into the deep water
and let down your nets for a catch."
Luke 5:4, NASB

Just imagine that you were Simon Peter. You'd fished all night and caught nothing. A rabbi is preaching to a crowd. You listen with both ears and an open heart, and something deep in you awakens. Jesus's words included the promise "for a catch." It was up to Peter to launch out again into deep water with his nets. This is where you are right now. Let your faith arise, and launch your dream. The dream in your heart is for your success, not failure.

So many years, Lord, of wondering, trying, and failing, with only some success. You've awakened the me *deep inside, and I'm beginning to let inspiration flow again. I've set aside doubt and unbelief for good. I'm ready to launch out with You into the deep water of the unknown. I do know this: You are with me, and it's for my good and those I love.*

Today I will let down my nets and fish with Jesus.

His Vision for Me

Where there is *no vision, the people perish.*
Proverbs 29:18, KJV

We use this Scripture to emphasize the importance of the end goal for projects, businesses, and even churches. The word "vision" is best translated as "divine revelation."[1] The Lord is calling you into your destined purpose. Every generation has unique experiences and qualities. We gain from those who have gone before us and give to those who follow us. Today is your day to ask the Lord for His vision for you. Get out a pad or journal. Sit quietly and ask Him, "What is Your vision for me?"

> *Here I am, Lord. Speak to me as I sit in Your presence with paper and pen. Give me a revelation of who I am and what You want me to do. I long to fully comprehend the Father's purpose for my life. I've quieted my thoughts and calmed my heart. I am here before You. Speak, Lord. Your handmaiden is listening. What is Your vision for me?*

Today I will write the Lord's vision for me.

For Such a Time

Who knows whether you have come
to the kingdom for such *a time as this?*
Esther 4:14, NKJV

We are familiar with Queen Esther's story and the moment she faced the hardest decision of her life. You may not be a queen standing in the gap for her people, but you are just as crucial to Father God. Your birth circumstances were God-planned. When, where, with whom—all of these factors have contributed to your identity. Add your spiritual gifts, skills and talents, and life experiences with God's perfect timing, and you now have the makings of a destined life.

Lord, don't pass me by! I accept Your proposal. I am ready, willing, and able to marry Your vision for my life. I take You, Jesus, to have and to hold from this day forward. I will love You, myself, and my fellow man as You have loved me. I pledge to serve You with all my heart as You enable me to do so.

Today I recognize my call for such a time as this.

July

HOW CAN I
IMPACT MY WORLD?

In America, we celebrate the adoption of our Declaration of Independence on the Fourth of July with fireworks, parades, and public displays of our flag and patriotism. As Christians, we are not only patriots of our nation; we are patriots of the kingdom of heaven. We declare our dependence on God. Our prayer circle expands this month because our confidence has grown. Just like firecrackers, our faith bursts into flame. We are passionate to see His will done on earth as in heaven.

Like Esther, you were born for such a time as this. God knew where you'd live, your neighbors, city, state, and nation. You were destined to be this age at this time. Have you ever wondered about that? Why me? Why now? Why not hundreds of years ago? Perhaps it's because God needed your personality, talents, giftings, and passion to serve His purpose today.

This month, it's time for expansion. You'll walk in bold, new territories and learn to live, pray, and declare outside the boundaries of your four walls.

Move Your Tent Pegs

JULY 1

Enlarge the place of your tent,
stretch your tent curtains wide, do not hold back;
lengthen your cords, strengthen your stakes.
Isaiah 54:2, NIV

Today's world has home alarms, video doorbells, car alarms, phones, and watches with SOS alarms. Everyone seems to be on alert for intrusion or violence. That may be true for our bodies but not for our spirits. As a mature woman of God, you know His protection, but your neighbors may not. Through prayer, you can expand your spiritual reach, especially to your neighbors and those close to you.

Father, I sit safely in my home. Thank You for Your protection. Not everyone in my neighborhood knows You as I do. Today, I stand in the gap in prayer for my neighbors. Release Your Spirit to draw them to Jesus. Release Your ministering angels. Protect their children and property from the evil one. Increase my influence with my neighbors. Let them see Your light shining through me.

Today I will enlarge my heart for my
neighbors through prayer.

Bearing Fruit

JULY 2

They are like trees planted along the riverbank,
bearing fruit each season. Their leaves never wither,
and they prosper in all they do.
Psalm 1:3, NLT

Consider where you've been planted. As believers, we carry the light of the Lord. It shines for all to see—even our neighbors. A smile, a wave, or an act of kindness can go a long way to spreading the joy of Jesus. This generous spirit also works at your local grocery store, gas station, and convenience store. People remember kind people. They will remember you, and those connections will bear fruit.

Holy Spirit, thank You for orchestrating opportunities for me to bear fruit for Your kingdom's sake in my neighborhood and local stores. Frequent stops mean frequent chances to impact the lives of others. Help me to be aware of people. Slow my day down so I can be more attentive to Your nudges. I long to bear fruit in every season and every occasion. Bring some people or faces to my mind to pray for them today.

Today I will pray that my neighbors
feel God's touch.

Authority to Trample

*I have given you authority to trample on snakes
and scorpions and to overcome all
the power of the enemy; nothing will harm you.*
Luke 10:19, NIV

Going for walks is a common practice for many. It's an excellent form of exercise to maintain a healthy weight, improve heart health, and reduce stress, among other benefits. More than that, it's a perfect opportunity to pray for marriages, families, finances, and salvation. You'll see things in the natural (messy yards, too many cars, and so on), but the Lord will also show you the atmosphere of your neighborhood and various homes. As you walk, ask for revelation and pray accordingly.

Jesus, I know You love my neighbors. You died for them too. As I walk and drive these streets, show me how to pray for them. Give me a revelation of the battles they fight. Show me the marriages in trouble, the children in rebellion, the finances in difficulty, and however else the enemy is causing pain in their lives. Make my heart like Yours for my neighbors.

**Today I will walk or drive in my
neighborhood and pray.**

God Bless America

JULY 4

Blessed is *the nation whose God* is *the LORD.*
Psalm 33:12, NKJV

On December 20, 1605, a hundred fifty settlers and forty seamen left England in three wooden boats. On April 26th, after a violent storm, they saw the coast of Virginia. Their leader, Reverend Robert Hunt, required the colonists to pray and fast for three days before setting foot on shore. Afterward, he planted a seven-foot cross with these words.

We do hereby dedicate this Land, and ourselves, to reach the people within these shores with the Gospel of Jesus Christ, and to raise up godly generations after us, and with these generations take the kingdom of God to all the earth. May this covenant of dedication remain to all generations, as long as this earth remains, and may this land, along with England, be evangelist to the world. May all who see this cross, remember what we have done here, and may those who come here to inhabit join us in this covenant and in this most noble work that the Holy Scriptures may be fulfilled. [1]

**Today I agree America shall be saved
and be a light to the world.**

Grace and Peace

JULY 5

Grace to you and peace from God our
Father and the Lord Jesus Christ.
Philippians 1:2, NKJV

We are extensions of God's grace and peace. Everywhere you go, you carry His light and His love. The question is, do you show it to everyone you meet? A simple smile and hello says, "I see you. I'm open to you." Follow that up with a brief comment about anything, and you've made contact with another person made in God's image. It may be that your hello is the only human interaction they have that day. You can be an instrument of grace and peace every day if you're available.

Father, open my eyes to see Your children from a different lens.
Help me to spot the lonely and discouraged. Slow my world down
so I can be impactful when I'm out in public. Nudge me when
someone is in need. Give me witty things to say. Help me to extend
grace and peace to strangers as You do.

Today I will be ready to share His grace and peace.

Love Your Neighbor

JULY 6

Jesus replied: "'Love the Lord your God with all your heart
and with all your soul and with all your mind.'
This is the first and greatest commandment.
And the second is like it: 'Love your neighbor as yourself.'"
Matthew 22:37–39, NIV

These two commandments are very familiar. The first is easy to understand and follow. The second may take some work. We know what Jesus said, and with all our hearts, we want to comply. But sometimes it's really tough. Let's face it. There are things we don't even like about ourselves or others. So, ask the Lord what He loves about you and your neighbor.

This commandment is a tough one, Jesus. Some people in my world aren't that lovable. And yet, I know You gave Your life for all of us. Help me see my neighbor through Your eyes. Give me Your compassion and insight on how to pray for them. Change me on the inside so I can love them as You do.

Today I will gain insight on how to
love myself and my neighbor.

Your Walkabout

Go, walk through the length and breadth
of the land, for I am giving it to you.
Genesis 13:17, NIV

Holy Spirit highlights the importance of His people's effect on the land they inhabit throughout the Old and New Testaments. Abram, Noah, Jacob, Moses, Joshua, David, Daniel, Esther, Deborah, Jesus, and Paul are only a few whose lives impacted their world because of where the Lord sent them. Your home and location are just as important to God. You are His light shining in a dark world. Ask the Lord to transform lives as you walk, bike, or drive in your neighborhood.

Lord, may my every step claim these households for Your kingdom's sake. May Your glory be seen in their homes. May families be reconciled, marriages healed, health restored, and destinies pursued. I accept my responsibility for the gift of these neighbors. Show me how I can minister to them in simple ways. Use my prayers to bless them with Your love and compassion.

Today I will be a light to my neighbors
through my prayers.

Peace for My City

JULY 8

*And seek the peace of the city where I have caused you
to be carried away captive, and pray to the LORD for it;
for in its peace you will have peace.*
Jeremiah 29:7, NKJV

When Babylon defeated Israel and sent them as captives, Jeremiah, the Lord's prophet, was grieved for his people. But the Lord gave him hope with His counsel to seek and pray for the peace of Babylon. You are a light to your city, just as your neighborhood. Never discount God's purpose for you in your location. Pray for its peace.

Lord, thank You for the privilege of praying for _____, my city. I ask for Your presence in every church where Your people gather. May Your blessing be on our homes, schools, businesses, and governments. Expose evil, deception, and any corruption that would hinder the power of Your love, presence, and prosperity in our midst. Set an angelic guard around this city, and may the Prince of Peace rule here.

Today I will pray for the peace of my city.

Train Up Our Children

JULY 9

Train up a child in the way he should go:
and when he is old, he will not depart from it.
Proverbs 22:6, KJV

President John F. Kennedy Jr. once said, "Children are the world's most valuable resource and its best hope for the future."[1] All generations should be involved in the education of our young. We have a divine responsibility in our own homes. Whether you have children, grandchildren, nephews, nieces, or neighbor kids, your prayers for their teachers and administrators are paramount to the child's success. This need for prayer is especially true in today's culture.

Oh Father, I recognize that children are our heritage and legacy. I appeal to heaven for Your intervention in our schools, colleges, and universities. Protect our children from demonic culture and ideologies. I bring every preschool, middle school, high school, and college in my area before You now. Expose any corruption of our children's minds. Awaken adults to hidden agendas, and give them the courage to fight the battle in school boards.

Today I will pray for my city's schools.

Righteous City Government

I urge you, first of all, to pray for all people.
Ask God to help them; intercede on their behalf,
and give thanks for them. Pray this way for kings
and all who are in authority so that we can live peaceful
and quiet lives marked by godliness and dignity.
1 Timothy 2:1–2, NLT

On a local level, Paul made it very plain to Timothy that we are responsible for praying for those in authority over us. Your prayers have tremendous power to establish heaven's kingdom on earth, especially where you are. City councils, the mayor's office, city parks and recreation, senior centers, and all administrative services benefit from your involvement and prayers.

Lord Jesus, all dominion in heaven, on earth, and under the earth is Yours. I ask that You grant wisdom to rule over my city. Cause our citizens to elect righteous leaders in government, judicial, school, and hospital boards. Help me to discern the right ones for the job when I vote. And once in office, help me to pray for them to lead well.

Today I will pray for my city's government
and administrative services.

Our Shepherds

Guard the good deposit that was entrusted to you—
guard it with the help of the Holy Spirit who lives in us.
2 Timothy 1:14, NIV

Blessed is the city with shepherds who love their flocks as Jesus does. They care for their members, and as they do, they enrich the atmosphere of their community. Of course, you love and appreciate your own pastor. But consider the effect of many pastors in unity for their city and surrounding areas. You can do the same. As your pastor guards you with prayer and Holy Spirit guidance, pray it forward with your own prayers.

Jesus, You are the Good Shepherd. I ask You to pour out Your Spirit on all who minister in my city. Protect their health, finances, and families as they care for Your flock. May they be inspired by Your Word and their intimate union with You as they seek You for their ministry. Give them Your heart for my community, and cause them to unite as one in You.

Today I will pray for my local pastors and their churches.

May We Prosper

JULY 12

*Beloved, I pray that you may prosper in all things
and be in health, just as your soul prospers.*
3 John 1:2, NKJV

Have you ever noticed how some cities seem impoverished while others seem to be flourishing? It's as if you can sense an atmosphere of hopelessness in one city and thriving in another. John speaks of prosperity in terms of the soul (mind, will, and emotions). In a sense, cities have a soul too. Just as you as an individual can thrive, so can a city. As light-bearers, your prayers can transform a city from darkness to light, especially when joined with other believers.

Holy Spirit, when the earth was formed, You hovered over the waters, breathing out life. I ask You now to come to my city. Bring a fresh, new wind to blow away any despair and hopelessness. Energize my city with Your fire. Invigorate us with Your wisdom. Create a fresh entrepreneurial spirit. Breathe new life into our businesses and services. Awaken my city.

Today I will pray for my city's prosperity.

First Responders

JULY 13

*Praise be to the Lord my Rock, who trains my hands
for war, my fingers for battle. He is my loving God and my
fortress, my stronghold and my deliverer, my shield,
in whom I take refuge, who subdues peoples under me.*
Psalm 144:1–2, NIV

As believers in Jesus Christ, our first response in an emergency is to call upon His name. He *is* our first response. Gratefully, our society has also developed professionals trained explicitly as law enforcement, firefighters, paramedics, and emergency medical technicians. They give their all, even their lives, if necessary. It takes courage, discipline, and compassion to serve their fellow man. Next time you hear a siren, offer a heartfelt prayer.

Father, I ask You to guard, guide, and protect all those serving my community in law enforcement, medical, and other emergency services. It takes a special calling to perform these duties. I ask that each one receive their training from You, and they first take refuge in You. Watch over their families. Protect them as they protect us.

Today I will pray for my city's first responders.

Heal Our Land

JULY 14

Do not pollute the land where you are.
Bloodshed pollutes the land, and atonement cannot be
made for the land on which blood has been shed,
except by the blood of the one who shed it.
Numbers 35:33, NIV

As difficult as it may be to understand, you may be reaping what was sown into your city's land before you even arrived. When Cain slew Abel, the Lord responded, *"The voice of your brother's blood cries out to Me"* (Genesis 4:10). Historically, the church has understood the importance of identifying and repenting for wrongs done to the land and its native people. Do you know the history of your city? Do some research and pray.

Father, I am grateful for the power of Your Son's substitutional sacrifice and His precious blood shed for me and all mankind. As a representative of my city, I ask forgiveness for any bloodshed or unrighteous dealings with its people and land. I ask You to cleanse this land so that Your blessing might fall upon all who dwell here.

Today I repent for any bloodshed or wrongdoing
in my city and ask for forgiveness.

My State's Motto

*All these are the twelve tribes of Israel, and this is what
their father said to them when he blessed them. He blessed
them, every one with the blessing appropriate to him.*
Genesis 49:28, NASB

We are familiar with the parting blessing Jacob (Israel) gave to his
twelve sons before his death. Each blessing was different and
specific to the son's nature and destiny. So it is with the individual
fifty states in the United States of America. You were planted in
your state for a divine purpose. Spend some time researching the
history of your state. Look up your state's motto, and turn it into a
prayer of blessing.

*Father, I am grateful to be a citizen of this nation and this state.
May my state's motto reflect Your intention for its land and people.
May our ideals express Yours. Cause the citizens of this state to be
in union with Your divine plan. I bless my state with Your protection
and providence.*

Today I will pray a blessing over my state and its motto.

Godly Leaders

Everyone must submit to governing authorities.
For all authority comes from God, and those in positions
of authority have been placed there by God.
Romans 13:1, NLT

Paul's counsel to the Roman Christians might seem harsh, especially in the midst of persecution. But remember Jeremiah's prophetic word to captive Israel to seek the peace of Babylon. Holy Spirit is speaking to us about the importance of yielding to authority but diligently praying for our representative government. Just as you pray for the peace of your home and city, your state's governing officials need your prayers too.

Mighty God, I am privileged to elect our government and judicial officials with my vote. Guide my decisions. I ask for godly men and women, filled with wisdom and skill, to be called into service in my state. Move on those You have anointed for these positions. And Father, I ask that they choose godly administrators under them. I pray for their salvation and that they hear Your voice and govern righteously.

Today I will pray for my state's elected officials.

Prosperous Industry

JULY 17

*Blessed are all who fear the Lord, who walk
in obedience to him. You will eat the fruit of your labor;
blessings and prosperity will be yours.*
Psalm 128:1–2, NIV

Most states have God-given natural resources that provide industry, employment, and prosperity. Highly skilled entrepreneurs have fathered telecommunication, technology, research, manufacturing, and mom-and-pop businesses that contribute to the well-being of all residents. *You* play a significant part in your state's prosperity. Your skill, talent, and work ethic contribute to its profitability as you fear the Lord and walk in obedience.

Father, thank You for the gifts You've given to my state. So many industries began because of Your endowment in this land in resources and people. I pray for CEOs, entrepreneurs, and small business owners. Grant them Your wisdom and strategies to succeed so that many benefit from jobs that provide for their families. Where there is lack, I ask for Your abundance. And, Lord, impress on them who the giver is and give back to You through tithes and offerings to bless many.

Today I will pray for industries and businesses in my state.

Heal Our Past

If we confess our sins, he is faithful and just
and will forgive us our sins and purify us
from all unrighteousness.
1 John 1:9, NIV

Believers worldwide understand the power of identifying and confessing past sins before the Lord. With humility and in prayer, we ask for the Lord's forgiveness. Why? So that His blessing can again flow to our land and people. As a believing citizen of your state, you have His authority to pray for your state and see God move on its behalf to restore righteousness.

Father, only You know the past evil that was done in my state. I am aware of some history and even some occurring now. I appeal to You on our behalf and ask for forgiveness. Cleanse my state of all wrongdoing. Use my prayer today to activate a spirit of repentance. Raise up leaders in all areas of influence, especially Your church, to champion Your cause. May Your goodwill once again flow from border to border.

**Today I will ask for forgiveness for past
and current sins in my state.**

United in Purpose

JULY 19

Now I urge you, brothers and sisters, *by the name
of our Lord Jesus Christ, that you all agree and that there
be no divisions among you, but that you be made complete
in the same mind and in the same judgment.*
1 Corinthians 1:10, NASB

Unity is a recurring theme throughout the Word. It applies to individuals, families, tribes, and even the church. Our biggest challenges today are competing philosophies, ideologies, and lifestyles—blue state vs. red state, liberal vs. conservative, socialist vs. capitalist, and so on. Leadership and education play a significant role in the overall temperament of the state. Unity starts with you and your prayers of agreement.

Jesus, on the night before You died, You prayed that we all be one, just as You and the Father are. I recognize the divider-in-chief as our greatest enemy of peace, unity, and purpose. Join my prayers to the praying church in my state. Move on our behalf. Bring revival to our churches and awakening to the lost. Raise up gifted leaders to encourage us.

**Today I will pray for unity of mind, judgment,
and purpose in my state.**

One of Fifty

He makes the whole body fit together perfectly.
As each part does its own special work, it helps the other
parts grow, so that the whole body is healthy
and growing and full of love.
Ephesians 4:16, NLT

Each state in our nation has peculiar characteristics. Rivers, mountains, deserts, forests, swamps, and plains define most. Consider your own family. You have shared DNA, and yet you are unique. The same applies to the God-defined and man-recognized borders of our states. Your state is one of fifty, but we are one nation under God. And so we pray for our states to fit together perfectly.

I thank You, Lord, that You have defined the borders of my state for a divine purpose. Our personality makes us unique with Your distinguished plans, purposes, and specific work. Grant that our government leaders and citizens work toward a healthy and growing state. You've called my state to fit harmoniously into this nation. Guide us into Your perfection.

**Today I will pray that my state does
its part for the whole.**

Reopen the Wells

Will You not revive us again,
That Your people may rejoice in You?
Psalm 85:6, NKJV

Since the First Great Awakening in 1734 and the Second Great Awakening in 1800, America has had repeated revivals that have swept every state. Some states have been blessed with many revivals. The initial locations of these revivals are called wells. Intercessors across the nation have prayed for these wells to reopen. You can do your part. Do an internet search of past revivals in your state, and ask the Lord to reopen the wells!

Lord Jesus, these past years have been very dry in my state. Some have drifted away from their active faith; others have never met the Savior of their souls. Send Holy Spirit's wind and fire to my state. Blow Your breath on us, and awaken our spirits. Fan the flame of faith. Ignite Your people with a passion for the lost. Cause the wells of revival to reopen and flow in my state.

Today I will pray that the wells of
revival reopen in my state.

Bless Our Nation

JULY 22

Save your people and bless your inheritance;
be their shepherd and carry them forever.
Psalm 28:9, NIV

After three days of prayer and fasting, on April 29, 1607, Reverend Robert Hunt and 105 English settlers planted a seven-foot wooden cross at Cape Henry, Virginia, and consecrated the land in covenant with God. America's four-hundred-year roots are still there. We have experienced many wars and tragedies but still stand as one nation under God. You are a citizen of this nation and chosen by God to inherit the blessing of this covenant. Pass it on.

Lord, continue to bless the United States of America. For hundreds of years, Americans took the gospel to the nations of the world. Reignite our passion to export the gospel, truth, compassion, generosity, and strength. Help us find our bearings again. Refocus our lives on You as our Lord and Savior. Help me in my generation to value those who have gone before me, and raise up those behind me to carry the torch of freedom and honor You as Lord.

Today I will pray that the United States
makes God their Lord.

Proclaim Liberty

JULY 23

*Proclaim liberty throughout all the land
unto all the inhabitants thereof.*
Leviticus 25:10, KJV

In 1751, the Speaker of the Pennsylvania Assembly commissioned the Liberty Bell for their state house and engraved this Scripture. The bell rang often from Independence Hall as a reminder of the liberty granted by William Penn for its citizens to make laws and the freedom to choose their religion. We are most fortunate to live in this nation. We should cherish our liberty and proclaim it often. What does liberty mean to you?

Father God, I am so grateful for my liberty in Jesus Christ. Surrendering my heart to Him has freed me from the tyranny of sin and evil. Your plan of salvation has written my name in the Book of Life for eternity. My heart is for all those who have yet to receive forgiveness and eternal life. Ring the bell loudly in their homes. Let them hear Your call. Awaken them to Your love. Give me opportunities to share Your message of liberty.

**Today I proclaim liberty to once again ring
throughout our land.**

For Freedom's Sake

JULY 24

It is for freedom that Christ has set us free.
Stand firm, then, and do not let yourselves
be burdened again by a yoke of slavery.
Galatians 5:1, NIV

April 12, 1864, our nation entered a Civil War that cost our country 620,000 lives over the abolition of slavery. That loss equals the number of lives lost in *all* wars, from the Revolutionary War to the Korean War.[1] If it's worth dying for freedom, it's worth praying for it to continue. We may experience external battles, but we have internal battles too. The freedom you've gained through salvation is worth fighting for.

Jesus, Your sacrifice on Calvary set humanity free from sin and death if we choose You over bondage. Lord, I have, and I do, still choose You this day. My heart grieves for my nation caught in the enemy's grip. War has cost many physical lives, but even more have lost their souls. Help me to stand and walk in the freedom Your sacrifice purchased for me and my nation.

Today I will pray for courage to stand firm in
the freedom Christ bought for me.

Three Branches

For the LORD is our judge, the LORD is our lawgiver,
the LORD is our king; he will save us.
Isaiah 33:22, KJV

Our King of kings and Lord of lords is all three branches in one. In wisdom, our founders established the judicial, legislative, and executive branches. Our Constitution formed our federal and state governments in such a way as to operate separately but equally for the good of its citizens. You can see this foundational principle in your own life as well. You reap the rewards from His executive authority, obedience to His laws, and recognition of His justice on earth.

Lord Jesus, I know You are returning to establish Your righteous kingdom on the earth, but You also encourage me to represent Your kingdom principles here and now in my nation. You taught us to pray, Your kingdom come and Your will be done on earth as it is in heaven. Today, let Your kingdom rule the hearts of my family, state, and nation.

Today I will pray for righteous justice,
laws, and governance.

Stability of Our Times

JULY 26

And He will be the stability of your times,
A wealth of salvation, wisdom, and knowledge;
The fear of the LORD is his treasure.
Isaiah 33:6, NASB

Picture a beautiful treasure chest before the throne of God. What do you suppose is inside? What promises and provisions are available to us? Now, reread the above verse. What is the key to stability, salvation, wisdom, and knowledge? It is the reverential fear of the Lord. He is compassionate, merciful, faithful, majestic, and all-powerful. If you want stability in your home, state, and nation, pray for the fear of the Lord to fall on all.

Loving Father and righteous God, I humble myself before You today for myself and my nation. I repent for taking You for granted. You are sovereign and rule with compassion, mercy, and justice. I ask You to pour out a spirit of repentance on our nation. We need to experience the reverential awe of Your presence. Lord, give us the key to Your treasure.

Today I will pray for the stability of
our times for my nation.

We Are His People

If my people, who are called by my name, will humble
themselves and pray and seek my face and turn from their
wicked ways, then I will hear from heaven, and I will
forgive their sin and will heal their land.
2 Chronicles 7:14, NIV

This verse is often quoted as an encouraging corporate prayer for
nations. Notice that it begins with *my* people, but it ends with *their*
land. Those who know the Lord and His ways are uniquely
qualified to stand in the gap for all. A little light dispels utter
darkness. A little leaven works the whole dough. A mustard seed
can grow to become a tree. Your prayer could tip the scales.

Gracious Father, Your ears are always open to the cry of my heart.
Forgive us for what Your people have allowed into our nation's
laws, culture, schools, and homes. I am convicted of my part and
ask forgiveness. Convict me of any hidden sin. Wash me clean.
Baptize me afresh with Your Spirit.

Today I will humble myself and pray for my nation.

Be My Anthem

But let all who take refuge in you rejoice; let them sing joyful praises forever. Spread your protection over them, that all who love your name may be filled with joy.
Psalm 5:11, NLT

Nothing is more inspiring than being in a stadium, at a parade, or watching a national event when we sing our nation's anthem. The patriot in you awakens, your spirit rises, and a joyful harmony seems to explode in joy. Similarly, something bursts inside when we worship and sing well-known songs. It's called love of country and love of our Lord. Make Him your anthem.

You are the Lord our banner, and Your banner over us is love. Thank You, God, for covering our nation. May my song of praise join others throughout this nation in honoring You. Father God, bless America. Guide, protect, and give us leaders who love and fear You in all areas of influence. You alone are our refuge. Keep us under Your watchful eye.

Today I will sing an anthem of thanksgiving to the Lord for my nation.

All the Earth

*All the ends of the earth will remember and turn
to the LORD, And all the families of the
nations will worship before You.*
Psalm 22:27, NASB

No matter the chaos in our world, the wars and rumors of wars, or the devastation of earthquakes and hurricanes, our God is on the throne. He rules with wisdom, truth, and justice. We have the privilege of praying for His compassion and mercy upon all the families in every nation. It begins first with the gospel. Let the faith in you spread from your neighborhood to your state and from your nation to your world.

Lord, Your greatest desire was and is for fellowship and intimacy with all Your created sons and daughters. I ask You, Lord, to cause this world to awaken to Your glorious presence. You once showed Your glory to Moses, and Jesus revealed His glory to John. It transformed them forever. That's my prayer, Lord. Show me Your glory. Inspire me so that I might inspire others.

**Today I will pray that all the earth awakens
to the glory of the Lord.**

The Lord Saves

Sing a new song to the LORD! Let the whole earth sing
to the LORD! Sing to the LORD; praise his name.
Each day proclaim the good news that he saves.
Psalm 96:1–2, NLT

What does the world need now? Love? Compassion? Mercy? This psalmist clearly states it's the good news of salvation. It begins with us and our circles of influence. As you capture the Lord's heart for family, you begin to see the bigger picture of His heart for the families of the world. Do you hear His heartbeat? Are you moved by news of drought, famine, wars, persecution? Sing a new song today, and proclaim His good news.

There is none like You, Lord, who can touch my heart and lift my spirits. Today, I ask You to lighten the atmosphere around the world. Let Your sun shine, Your soft winds blow, and Your gentle rains fall on Your children. Whatever the need, let Your sons and daughters in the earth see, hear, and know Your good news.

Today I will sing a new song and
proclaim the good news.

Reign Forever

JULY 31

The seventh angel sounded his trumpet, and there
were loud voices in heaven, which said: "The kingdom
of the world has become the kingdom of our Lord and of his
Messiah, and he will reign for ever and ever."
Revelation 11:15, NIV

Long ago, when you acknowledged Jesus Christ as your Lord and Savior, your name was written in the Book of Life. Holy Spirit planted eternity in your heart and spirit forever. Nothing can rob you of that unless you walk away from truth. The day is coming when the whole world will see Him as you do. As we complete this month, rejoice, daughter of the King!

My heart is full, Jesus. You are indeed my King of kings and Lord
of lords. As I have prayed for my neighborhood, state, nation, and
Your world, I have gained a great appreciation for Your heart for
every one of us. Lord, use my prayers to increase Your light in my
world. Send revival. Pour Your Spirit out on a thirsty world.

Today I will pray for a worldwide revival.

WHAT IS MY IMPORTANCE TO OTHERS?

God made you to be an integral component of many lives. Picture a unicycle wheel. You are the center hub that connects everyone in your sphere of influence. When the bike is in motion, the spokes turn with you. Now picture Jesus on the seat with His feet on the pedals and hands on the steering wheel. His pedaling initiates Holy Spirit wind and fire; you're moving in His flow.

Praying women never vacation, but we must pull away for rest and relaxation. When we do, inspiration flows, opportunities arise, and divine appointments will surely come our way. Busy lives and stress can lead to a loss of togetherness. That's why deliberate focus is essential, especially with our families. The lazy days of summer are ending, but what we do now prepares us for a harvest of answered prayers and declarations.

This month, you will begin focusing on those nearest to you: spouses, significant friendships, children and grandchildren, and church family. You'll then expand that circle of influence with your generation and, finally, the aging and the young.

Rest in Presence

My Presence will go with you,
and I will give you rest.
Exodus 33:14, NKJV

You are the most important person in many lives. You give your all at whatever work you do. You keep your home running smoothly and care for the needs of everyone. So, how can you manage to do that on your own? You can't. Even the depleted need to be reenergized. Moses had an impossible task to lead Israel into the Promised Land, and he doubted his ability. God's reply was the key: His presence brings His rest.[1]

Father, I recognize the importance of caring for me before I can care for anyone else. I want to be present for everyone in the weeks ahead, but I will need a mega dose of presence from You. As I step away for quiet time with You, meet me with Your goodness. Infuse my heart with Your love. Heal my body of any disorder or disjointedness. Feed my spirit with Yours, and cleanse my soul.

Today I will rest in His presence.

Heart of the Matter

AUGUST 2

The heart of her husband trusts in her,
And he will have no lack of gain.
She does him good and not evil All the days of her life.
Proverbs 31:11–12, NASB

Not all women are married, but most have a significant other in their lives at one time or another. In this verse, the "heart" translates as the inner man.[1] Trust is the basis of every covenantal relationship. That means when you trust God, it extends to your covenant relationship with your husband and other significant relationships. Covenant is why God is constantly wooing you into His presence with His goodness. And the goodness you experience, you extend to others.

Thank You for yesterday's quiet time with You, Lord. Today, I ask You to show me my covenant relationships. Am I giving my all? Do You see Your goodness to me flowing to them? Help me to be generous with my time and resources to love them as well as You do. I bless them today with Your love and protection.

Today I will practice goodness toward my
spouse or someone close to me.

Love Is...

AUGUST 3

Love is patient, love is kind. It does not envy,
it does not boast, it is not proud.
1 Corinthians 13:4, NIV

We quote the apostle Paul's definition of love often. We see it on t-shirts, coffee cups, and plaques. What is your definition of love? Patience is easy, like holding back anger or frustration, but maybe that's more like *self*-control. What about kind? Perhaps it's going out of your way to do something nice. Again, the *self* is involved. The negatives—envy, boasting, and pride—are easy to define and avoid with the Holy Spirit's help. Spend some time thinking about how you can love a little more.

Father, I'm thinking about Your love and how patient and kind You are with me every day. I sense Your pleasure when I'm at peace. I can flow with Your grace most of the time, but there are days when I just need an extra ounce from You poured into me. Fill me up to overflowing today.

Today I will look for ways to be especially patient and kind.

Winsome Ways

AUGUST 4

Be an example to all believers in what you say,
in the way you live, in your love, your faith, and your purity.
1 Timothy 4:12, NLT

We are always being observed, even when we don't think so. In this verse, Paul counseled Timothy on how to conduct himself with his flock. Paul wrote to the Corinthian church that they were epistles read by everyone.[1] Now think of those closest to you, not just the general public. What is the message you are expressing in words and deeds? Is His grace in you winning some to Jesus?

Holy Spirit, You know me better than I know myself. The Word says that I am an epistle that people read. What is the message I am giving out to the people around me? I long to live a righteous life filled with love and winsome ways to attract people to You, Lord. Could You read me today? How am I doing? Are there areas where I need a little more light?

Today I will evaluate my ways with others.

Presence Carriers

AUGUST 5

*When they saw the courage of Peter and John
and realized that they were unschooled, ordinary men,
they were astonished and they took note that
these men had been with Jesus.*
Acts 4:13, NIV

We all know people who light up the room when they walk in. It's like they carry fragrant sunshine with happy bubbles floating around them. That's a tell-tale sign of joy, peace, rest, and Jesus. Peter and John were ordinary fishermen, but they were emboldened by experiencing the presence of Jesus, their faith, and the empowerment of Holy Spirit. You can be emboldened too.

Lord Jesus, more than anything, I want to know You and experience what Peter and John did after Pentecost. Holy Spirit transformed them from hiding in an upper room with a few people to standing before thousands, preaching the good news after He visited them. I want to do that too. Pour out Your Spirit on me as I spend my quiet time with You today. May I carry Your fragrance everywhere I go.

Today I will seek His presence and be filled to overflowing.

Collaborators in Glory

AUGUST 6

*The one who plants and the one who waters
have one purpose, and they will each be rewarded
according to their own labor.*
1 Corinthians 3:8, NIV

We don't go through life as "us four and no more." The Father made us to be in the midst of others. Families, classrooms, workspaces, committees, and even special interest groups have one thing in common. Some are leaders, some are followers, some are servers, and some just show up. We are all colaborers with Christ. There are gifts in you that no one else can bring. Your design has an impact on the lives of others and vice versa.

Father, You designed me. Jesus, You gave me access. Holy Spirit, You made deposits in me. Please forgive me for only looking at myself and what I bring to the table. Open my eyes to see Your design and gifts in others. Help me to draw them out so they can shine. I want to serve others in whatever capacity You've called me to.

Today I will learn to collaborate well with others.

Grace to Endure

And let endurance have its *perfect result,*
so that you may be perfect and complete, lacking in nothing.
James 1:4, NASB

Endurance sounds so negative, doesn't it? Other translations say perseverance, steadfastness, or patience.[1] "Perfect" means reaching the goal or full grown, age, or maturity in Christ.[2] So, what do most of us have to endure to reach perfection? Most of us would say *who* is the better word. That's right. It's people in your life. They know your nature, what buttons to push, even when you'll cave or take a stand. So does the Lord, and He loves to pour His grace on you.

Lord, only You know what I have to endure—family, work, me, we, and they *issues. You know them all. All I can say is thank You. Your grace is always perfect for me. I trust You to work Your perfection in me so that I can be perfect in my responses to all in my life. We're in this together. I lack nothing in You.*

Today I will have His grace to endure and lack nothing.

Nurture Our Children

AUGUST 8

May our sons flourish in their youth like well-nurtured plants.
May our daughters be like graceful pillars,
carved to beautify a palace.
Psalm 144:12, NLT

The Father has created a beautiful world of natural resources and a fruitful land. But more than our environment, He has given us the ability to reproduce ourselves. We see our children as our fruits. We delight in pouring all the knowledge we have gained into them, hoping they will go beyond our successes. Whether you have children or not, the Lord calls you to teach them by your example. You have the potential to nurture them into their calling and purpose.

Jesus, You were always passionate about the children, calling them to You for blessing. You taught us to pray to Your Father and ours as Abba. Help me to maintain a childlike attitude of wonder and trust in You. Grant me wisdom, knowledge, and grace to raise the next generation to know and fear the Lord and love You as I do.

Today I will pray for all children to know their God.

Teach Them Well

All your children will be taught by the LORD,
and great will be their peace.
Isaiah 54:13, NIV

What a promise! When we dedicate our children to the Lord and raise them to know and love Him, the Lord joins us every step of the way. Just as He is for you, He is for them. Every child is unique to Him with His distinct attributes and a divine purpose, just like yours. It is a privilege to mentor them in their callings and life purposes. The result is their peace. It's not just perfect. It's complete, especially with your partnership.

Thank You, Lord, for the privilege of fostering Your children here on earth. Whether they belong to my family or others, You perfectly designed each child for a divine purpose. Help me see their potential, spot Your gifts, and encourage them. Young adults face many social issues today. I ask for wisdom and grace to listen well and communicate respectfully and truthfully.

Today I will partner with the Lord in
teaching our children.

Shepherding with Care

AUGUST 10

*He will feed his flock like a shepherd. He will carry
the lambs in his arms, holding them close to his heart.
He will gently lead the mother sheep with their young.*
Isaiah 40:11, NLT

In Numbers 14, we learn that children aren't adults until they're twenty. That's two decades of destiny-building to shape their faith and provide opportunities to develop their gifts and abilities. Even if you don't have children, your interactions do affect them. You are partnering with a doting, gentle, loving Father who adores His kids.

*Your Father's heart for our children is so tender, Lord. I can see
You carrying them and holding them close to Your heart, protecting
them from danger. Lord, I ask for insight on how best to interact
with and mentor these precious children. I understand my
responsibility and ask for grace to lead and guide them. Help me to
communicate truth in simple ways, just as Jesus did.*

Today I will seek gentle ways to impact the lives of children.

Come Home!

So he returned home to his father.
And while he was still a long way off, his father
saw him coming. Filled with love and compassion,
he ran to his son, embraced him, and kissed him.
Luke 15:20, NLT

We all know family and extended family members who have either never come to faith or left the faith. Our hearts break for them. Some have slipped into such a downward spiral that we wonder if they'll ever receive the Father's love through the saving knowledge of Jesus Christ. You aren't alone in your grief. Great is the love of God and the power of God through your impactful prayers to bring them home.

Jesus, You are the Way, the Truth, and the Life.[1] No one comes to the Father except through You. I ask You to open their eyes to see, ears to hear, and hearts to understand Your great love for them. May Your kingdom come near them, heal their souls, revive their spirits, and awaken them to the Father's love and compassion.

Today I will pray for prodigals to come home.

Our Crowning Glory

Grandchildren are the crowning glory of the aged;
parents are the pride of their children.
Proverbs 17:6, NLT

You may or may not have children and grandchildren, but we can all agree that children are the future. We understand the importance of legacy, or leaving the world touched by our lives in some way or another. You have a gift to give those who will rise up after you. It doesn't need to be a physical trait. It can be the impact of your mentoring and acknowledging their worth that will eventually establish their own legacy.

Lord, thank You for all of the children in my life. Help me to see them as You do. Give me a heart to help them in their growth and maturity. I desire to see all of the generations honoring one another. I know that would please You as You love to bless our children and children's children. May my life have a ripple effect on their lives to Your glory.

Today I will pray about the legacy
of love I am creating.

Giving Honor

Honor your father and mother.
Then you will live a long, full life in the land
the LORD your God is giving you.
Exodus 20:12, NLT

The fifth commandment is the only commandment with a blessing promised. The Lord tells us we will reap what we sow in obedience and honor to our parents. The Hebrew word for "long" means to grow and continue long.[1] Like yesterday, it implies legacy. You receive God's favor when you honor your parents, even when they are undeserving. Don't you believe God's heart is the same for us to honor His children?

Lord, Your Word tells us to honor and respect everyone, especially parents, even if they are undeserving. Sometimes, it's really hard, Lord. Of course, I could walk away or avoid them because of my disapproval, but that doesn't reflect Your love very well. I'm asking for greater grace for these situations, Lord. Show me how to love and honor all the generations.

Today I will look for ways to give honor to all generations.

Our Heritage

Behold, children are *a heritage from the LORD,*
The fruit of the womb is *a reward.*
Psalm 127:3, NKJV

Why is heritage important? We are building an ever-increasing kingdom. You are an essential part of Jesus's heritage. Your faith has brought you in as a daughter of the King. You now play an integral role in bringing His kingdom to earth. The children you bear and nurture into His kingdom increase His presence in the world. And those who mentor others' children share the same heritage. Eternal rewards await you.

What a privilege it is, Jesus, to partner with You in bringing Your kingdom to earth. May heaven's will be done in my family and in my circles of influence. Lord, I long to lead my children and grandchildren, as well as those of others, into a saving knowledge and fruitful life in You. Your reward is my reward. Help me to see their potential and encourage them to fulfill their destinies.

Today I will pray for a fruit-filled heritage.

Stand in Prayer

AUGUST 15

*Therefore put on the full armor of God, so that when
the day of evil comes, you may be able to stand your
ground, and after you have done everything, to stand.*
Ephesians 6:13, NIV

We're almost three-quarters through the year, and you've set your
stakes in the ground, standing firm in faith and declaring God's will
on the earth for you, your family, and your circles of influence.
When you take off in flight, they always warn you to put on your
oxygen mask before the child's mask. The same is true in spiritual
warfare for our children. Put on your armor and then stand for them.

*Father, I thank You that Your Word has prepared and positioned me
to put on Your full armor and take a stand for these next
generations. Empower me with spiritual knowledge and
discernment of the evil that influences our children. Embolden me
to stand and fight along Your side through my prayers.*

Today I will take a stand in prayer for our children.

Anointed Pastors

AUGUST 16

Preach the word of God. Be prepared, whether the time
is favorable or not. Patiently correct, rebuke,
and encourage your people with good teaching.
2 Timothy 4:2, NLT

Pastors probably have the most challenging roles of the fivefold ministry gifts to the church. They organize, administrate, deal with finances and boards, counsel, study, pray, marry and bury, and deliver timely messages to their flocks. On top of that, they deal with their own marriages and families. You are an essential support to your pastor, and you do that through prayer.

Jesus, I ask that You disciple pastors. Let them encounter You often.
Keep them filled with Your Spirit. Breathe on them as they read
Your Word. Holy Spirit, I ask for illumination and revelation.
Inspire them as they seek You for their congregations. May they
preach Your Word with boldness. May they partner with Holy Spirit
to open our eyes and ears and ignite our hearts with their
leadership. May signs, wonders, and miracles follow their
preaching.

Today I will pray for my pastor.

One Big Family

Dear brothers and sisters, I close my letter
with these last words: Be joyful. Grow to maturity.
Encourage each other. Live in harmony and peace.
Then the God of love and peace will be with you.
2 Corinthians 13:11, NLT

One of the definitions of a family is all the descendants of a common ancestor. All who believe, across this world and as far back as the resurrection, are joined by one immutable truth: everyone who calls on the name of Jesus will be saved.[1] Belonging to a fellowship is more than showing up on Sunday. It's a blood-washed commitment to family.

Lord, today I want to give thanks for every man, woman, and child in my church. I am so grateful for their friendship and fellowship. Lord, I pray that the family of God that meets each Sunday will be vibrant with life, love, and joy. May the families be in one accord, honoring each other. May the love we share flow to our communities and the lost, the least, and the hurting.

Today I will pray for my church family.

In One Accord

When the day of Pentecost came,
they were all together in one place.
Acts 2:1, NIV

The humble beginnings of our Christian faith began when 120 disciples went to the upper room to pray together in unity and wait for the promised baptism of the Holy Spirit. Ten days later, the Holy Spirit filled them on Pentecost; the rest is history. The *church* has undergone many transitions and seasons since the first century. But one thing is timeless and without question: the power of agreement, especially in prayer.

Lord, there is much power in agreement. I pray for my church but for so much more. I ask You to unite the churches in my city. As leaders in the body of Christ, cause them to desire to meet and take a stand for righteousness in our community. Anoint them with Your wisdom and strategy that Your body might unite under Your headship to impact our city and, by extension, our county, state, and nation.

Today I will pray for the churches in
my city to be in one accord.

We're Not Abandoned

As a shepherd cares for his flock on a day when he is among his scattered sheep, so I will care for My sheep and will rescue them from all the places where they were scattered on a cloudy and gloomy day.
Ezekiel 34:12, NASB

As we consider our church family and the flocks scattered worldwide, we are encouraged by the Lord's careful watch. We relish our freedom here, but many worldwide are persecuted or hidden. As this new era of technology and global societal changes occur, we can become discouraged and even fearful. That's all the more reason for you to stay close to the Lord and fellowship.

Jesus, You are our Great Shepherd and soon-coming King. In these days of global turmoil and chaos, show me how to pray with confidence for the persecuted church, the unsaved, and the saved. I trust in Your mercy and compassion as well as Your justice. Your wisdom is far beyond mine, but You delight in showing me my part.

Today I will pray for the persecuted church.

Linked Hearts

*And may the Lord make you increase and abound in love
to one another and to all, just as we* do *to you.*
1 Thessalonians 3:12, NKJV

Have you ever noticed how we tend to cluster when we gather at church functions? We have a kindred sister spirit with some women. That's the nurturing effect the Lord has on His flock. We meet others with the same interests in ministry, Bible study, raising children, and even bargain shopping. He knows what you need and provides opportunities to link our hearts. They are the sisters you call when you need the hands and feet of God on earth.

*Lord, I am so grateful for the women in my church. They are open
to friendship, caring for me, and supportive. I know that You are
working through them for my benefit. I ask that You bless them and
their families as much as they bless me. Show me ways to widen the
circle and link my heart to them and others.*

Today I will pray for my spiritual sisters.

A Gifted Saint

The human body has many parts,
but the many parts make up one whole body.
So it is with the body of Christ.
1 Corinthians 12:12, NLT

We spent the first part of this year focusing on your unique identity, the *me* God created you to be. Today, let's focus on you as part of the *we*. The Lord established the fivefold ministry for the equipping of the saints. Holy Spirit has proportionally given nine unique gifts and seven motivational gifts.[1] All of these gifts are to build up the body of Christ. You are the beneficiary of many of these gifts. Do you know what they are, and are you using them?

Lord, You have enabled me to be an integral part of Your body here on earth. Help me to understand what gifts You have deposited in me. Open the eyes of my understanding, and bring revelation for Your kingdom's purpose for my life. I don't want to waste anything You have freely given me.

Today I will begin to understand
Holy Spirit's gifts in me.

They Get Me

AUGUST 22

Be filled with the Spirit, speaking to one another
with psalms, hymns, and songs from the Spirit.
Sing and make music from your heart to the Lord.
Ephesians 5:18–19, NIV

No matter what age we are, we have a particular affinity for those of our generation. We simply *get* what has been, what is, and what will be. Most of us marry, have children, struggle through their education years, and launch them into their own marriages. What would you do without the support of your spiritual sisters in this process? They *get* you and know how to pray with and for you.

Today, Lord, I want to thank You for the cherished Christ-filled friends I have in my life. They know when to sit in silence or speak a word of encouragement at just the right time. Bless my dear friends with more of You in their lives. Bless the work You've called them to. Nudge me to pray for them in times of hidden need. Bind us together in unity by Your Spirit.

Today I will pray for my generation.

Serve God's Purpose

For David, after he had served his own generation
by the will of God, fell asleep, was buried with his fathers.
Acts 13:36, NKJV

How do you define generation? It could be only those of your age group. Or it could be all who are alive at the same time you are. Looking at the more comprehensive definition, it includes your parents and grandparents ahead of you as well as the children and grandchildren behind you.[1] You have a significant impact on both. Consider yourself a bridge, joining all generations with you as the link. Now, do you understand God's purpose for your importance to both?

Lord, I recognize that You have placed me here and now for Your divine purpose. With all my heart, I want to serve not only those of my age group but also my elders and those younger than me. Give me Your heart's understanding. Help me to honor them by honoring You in them. Open my eyes to see them as You do.

Today I will serve God's purpose for this generation.

Who Will?

AUGUST 24

Repeat them again and again to your children.
Talk about them when you are at home and when you are
on the road, when you are going to bed
and when you are getting up.
Deuteronomy 6:7, NLT

If we don't teach the next generation, who will? If we don't model Christian morals and virtue, who will? If we don't share our testimonies, who will? If others don't pass on the promises of God, will you? You are a woman of grace and beauty, uniquely gifted by God to impact your world today and future generations. What you teach, model, and share with the younger generations will live on after you.

Lord, You are loving and compassionate. You are great and greatly to be praised. Mark my life as one who honors you with my worship. Let all generations hear me praise You and bring You glory. The joy of You in my life is my strength. Use me to encourage all with my testimony of Your greatness. I delight in You, Lord, and I want all to see You as I do.

Today I will praise the Lord and
encourage others to join me.

Seeding for the Future

Our children will also serve him.
Future generations will hear about
the wonders of the Lord.
Psalm 22:30, NLT

You may be the very first believer in your family. Or you may be fortunate to come from a rich heritage of believers. In either case, you carry a wealth of resources within you. It doesn't even matter whether you have children or not. You have a weighty responsibility to pass on what you have to the next generation. When you gather, see, hear, and observe them. Let them know you do. Speak His life into theirs.

Father, I am privileged to know so many people of various ages. From toddlers to teens and beyond, I enjoy watching them grow and mature. I feel a responsibility to support their parents and encourage the youth. May they see my love for You and be encouraged that there is wonder in knowing the Lord at my age and every age.

Today I will encourage the young with
my love for the Lord.

Pour Your Spirit Out

And afterward, I will pour out my Spirit on all people.
Your sons and daughters will prophesy, your old men will
dream dreams, your young men will see visions.
Joel 2:28, NIV

Those of us who are middle-aged and beyond have seen significant changes in our nation and the world since the last century. Schools without prayer, abortion on demand, and today's lawlessness cry out for Holy Spirit's fire to again fall on us. Evil has taken a foothold, but you know Christ, our cornerstone. Your prayers to activate this promised outpouring for all generations can change the world.

Lord, I appeal to You for this generation. We are in desperate need of Your intervention in all areas of culture. From homes and families to churches and our government, we need a great awakening to release Your Spirit. Join my prayers to those around the world. Touch our hearts again. Awaken Your church to stand up and speak up. Set hearts on fire for You and start with mine.

Today I will ask Holy Spirit to pour
out His Spirit on us.

An Appeal to Heaven

AUGUST 27

But the mercy of the LORD is from everlasting
to everlasting for those who fear Him,
And His justice to the children's children.
Psalm 103:17, NASB

The Lord is tenderhearted toward His daughters. He understands your emotions, your needs, and your desires. He's placed a deposit of His nurturing nature in you for His purposes. The instinct to protect, guide, and mother is in your DNA. This gift is not just for your descendants but for all ages. You are a perfect intercessor to call upon His mercy and justice. He made your heart to mirror His.

Lord, thank You for knowing my heart and hearing my heart's cry. I have peace when I pray to You, even when chaos surrounds me. I believe You will answer my petitions for mercy and justice. Today, I don't ask for myself but for the children of the world. Poverty, war, famine, and political upheaval are rampant. I cry out for Your protection for the helpless and hopeless.

Today I will appeal to heaven for
the helpless and hopeless.

Peace Be Within

For the sake of my family and friends,
I will say, "Peace be within you."
Psalm 122:8, NIV

Everyone has a sense of what peace looks or feels like. It might be sitting quietly out at a lake, soaking in a hot bath, or having the house all to yourself. It's a time when you center yourself without extraneous stimuli. Everything is quiet within you. That's the moment to take a deep breath and exhale all the burdens of the day, week, or even month. In this moment, the Lord meets your core. And from that place, you can now pray His peace for others.

Lord, I often seem to be the run-to person with other people's problems. I'm happy to listen and counsel as needed. Sometimes I'm the actual problem-solver. But, Lord, I don't know what I would do without the peace You give me. I want You to know how grateful I am for our relationship. You are my hiding place. Help me to lead others to Your peace.

**Today I will release His peace to
my family and friends.**

Faithful to All

Your faithfulness endures *to all generations;*
You established the earth, and it abides.
Psalm 119:90, NKJV

There is such a powerful benefit in remembering. Suggestion: Take a yellow pad and pen. Write out the decades you've lived through on separate pages. Ask the Lord to show you significant events and His view at the time. (Remember, He never leaves or forsakes you, even in the most horrible times.) Now, fill in the blanks. What were the lessons learned? How did you grow and mature? What testimony do you have to share with others? Consider asking the older and younger generations for their testimonies.

Oh, blessed trinity—Father, Son, and Spirit—I am in awe of Your closeness to me. In my mind's eye, I see myself as a little girl, a teenager, my first love, and even my first job. Going down memory lane with You is precious. I especially remember the day I asked You into my heart. You were always with me. I just didn't know it until that day.

Today I will praise the Lord's faithfulness to me and all.

Rock Solid

But solid food belongs to those who are of full age,
that is, *those who by reason of use have their senses*
exercised to discern both good and evil.
Hebrews 5:14, NKJV

Ladies, we're way past the age of reason. We've paid our dues and graduated from the school of hard knocks. It's no more watered-down faith. It's full-bodied faith now. The older generation is counting on you to help them age gracefully. The younger generation is counting on you to keep them on the right path. The good news is you're ready! The Lord has been pouring His wisdom into you for decades. You stand on solid rock.

Holy Spirit, You have been a faithful companion and teacher all these years. You've opened the Scriptures to greater understanding. You've shown me how words written thousands of years ago are still pertinent today. Your Word has positively become a lamp to my feet. I'm ready for more, Lord. May Your wisdom increase in me so I might lead others with Your knowledge and revelation.

Today I ask for greater revelation
as I read Your Word.

Love Perfected

AUGUST 31

Love has been perfected among us in this:
that we may have boldness in the day of judgment;
because as He is, so are we in this world.
1 John 4:17, NKJV

How fortunate we are to have Holy Spirit dwelling within. He convicts, cajoles, leads, and loves. He's sent assigned angels to watch over and minister to you. He's given you His Word to inform and inspire. He's led you to wise models and mentors. He's birthed His fire in your heart and released living water from your spirit. This is your day and hour to be bold. His love is perfected in you.

Your perfect love drives out all my fear. You have made me fearless,
Lord. I know the woman You've created me to be, and I know this is
my time to be here in this world. Let Your light shine even greater
in me. Give me boldness for my family and peers and wisdom for
the elderly and the young.

Today I will declare His love is perfected in me.

September

WHAT IS GOD'S ASSIGNMENT FOR ME?

As students return to school, Bible studies, fellowship groups, and other outside activities start again in the fall. It is a perfect opportunity to hit the books and fill your quiver with new arrows. We acquire knowledge through exposure to new ideas and new mentors. Opportunities abound with conferences, whether in person or by live streaming on podcasts, Facebook, and YouTube channels. It's time to stretch yourself. Ask the Lord for His supernatural school assignment for you.

It takes nine months of pregnancy to produce a healthy child. You've been faithful these past months, the delivery has taken place, and you're ready for advanced growth and more responsibility. These next four weeks, you will spend time in the Word of God, join others in prayer, and review your prayer journal and what God is saying specifically to you. At the end of the month, you'll be ready to craft your own declarations and be open to any assignment the Lord is leading you to.

God's Word Is True

God is not a man, that He should lie, Nor a son of man,
that He should repent. Has He said, and will He not do?
Or has He spoken, and will He not make it good?
Numbers 23:19, NKJV

This month, we start from a place of certainty. If you believe in
Jesus Christ, the Word, then it's settled. Everything written in the
Bible is for your understanding and growth. You began with milk,
but now it's time for meat. His words and promises are true. Ask the
Spirit of truth to take you on a new journey.

Holy Spirit, You are a gift to me. When I recognized my sins and
asked for forgiveness, Jesus became my Savior, and You became my
teacher and constant companion. We have been on a journey since
that day. Today, I am asking You to take me to a new level of
revelation and understanding of Your Word. We could start at the
beginning or wherever You like.

Today Holy Spirit will guide me to what
I need to read in His Word.

Your Life Verse

I wait for the LORD, my whole being waits,
and in his word I put my hope.
Psalm 130:5, NIV

A life verse is a Scripture from the Word of God that rocks you to the core. It's like a promise made directly from heaven to your spirit and soul. You just know in your knower that this particular verse is for you. It becomes a power-packed, faith-fulfilling statement of divine fact. No one, no outside influence, and no circumstance can rob you of it. So, do you have one? Say it out loud. If you don't have one, ask Holy Spirit to lead you to your life verse.

Lord, I am so grateful that Your Word is clear, affirming, and full of rich wisdom. I love reading the Bible with You, Holy Spirit. I especially enjoy David's psalms, Jesus's story in the Gospels, and Paul's letters. I love putting my name in the Scriptures, like John 3:16, for God so loved me that He gave His one and only Son.

Today I will rejoice in my life verse.

Seek Him Early

SEPTEMBER 3

Seek the LORD while He may be found;
Call upon Him while He is near.
Isaiah 55:6, NASB

In today's world, "busyness" has become a byword. The world is speeding up, distractions are everywhere, and time-wasters abound. Here's the deal. You are the master of your time clock. Why not have breakfast with the King of your heart? Your Lord longs for intimate time with you. He wants to speak His heart into your day and gently guide you on your long-term path. Give Him your morning, and you'll find that you float through the rest.

I choose You first. I love the quiet of my mornings with You, Lord. I enjoy being open and honest about what's on my heart for myself and others. You are my Prince of Peace, Jesus. Sharing my needs and plans lifts the burdens off my shoulders and places them on Yours. While I work through my day, I am grateful that You are interceding for me. What a love exchange this is!

Today and every day, I will seek the Lord early.

At My Midday

Commit everything you do to the LORD.
Trust him, and he will help you.
Psalm 37:5, NLT

We are fortunate to have deep roots that hold us securely in place. Our faith in His Word is our anchor—no matter what storms we face. As you go about your day with errands, work, and endless projects, let your mind float back to the Scriptures you've been reading. What has Holy Spirit been highlighting? Daniel sought the Lord morning, noon, and night. Make that precious connection as you commit your day to Him. Take a breather at your midday, and let Him hear your praise.

As I progress through my day, Lord, with all that's on my plate to accomplish, meet me here as I step aside for this moment of reflection. I want You to accompany me all through my day. I take in a deep breath now and breathe in Your life-giving Spirit. Permeate my whole body with Your life. Restore my energy for the rest of my day. I trust You to help me through.

Today I will commit my focus and energy to the Lord.

Wackadoodle Days

Submit yourselves, then, to God. Resist the devil,
and he will flee from you. Come near to God
and he will come near to you.
James 4:7–8, NIV

One of the lasting benefits of putting the Word of God high on your daily priority list is the grace and courage it provides during your day. We all face unforeseen circumstances, whether it's an urgent call from a friend, something breaking down at home, or upheaval at work. You may have your day all planned, and it goes wacky. It's precisely at these times when the peace you gain in your time with the Lord gives you the opening to hear His guidance when needed.

Nothing takes You by surprise, Lord. But for me, some of my days can be unreal with their challenges. It means so much to me to commit each day to you. I hear Your voice, feel Your nudge, and even sense Your wisdom rising up in me. You have a marvelous way of refocusing my efforts. Thank You.

Today I will come near and stay near to God.

Teach Me, Lord

Teach me your way, LORD, that I may rely on your
faithfulness; give me an undivided heart,
that I may fear your name.
Psalm 86:11, NIV

Whatever we set our hearts to accomplish, if there is to be any fruit, we need to rely on the Lord. It begins with a reverential awe of God, who created the universe and you! He delights in your undivided commitment to Him, His Word, and His ways. When you open your heart and mind to understand the Scriptures, He unlocks wisdom and strategies that make you more than a conqueror.

Holy Spirit, be my highlighter today as I read Your Word. Underscore key words to activate what You're teaching me. Write on the margins of my heart what You want me to grab hold of. Turn the pages of my mind to bring me back to the point You're trying to make. Teach me all about Your ways. I want to know You just as You know me.

Today I will read the Word with illumination.

His Word Lights My World

SEPTEMBER 7

Your word is *a lamp to my feet And a light to my path.*
Psalm 119:105, NKJV

As we end these seven days honoring the Word and its daily importance, it's time to upgrade. Everyone is heading back to school this month. So, here is your challenge. Take your life verse and look up the Hebrew or Greek words in an online concordance. Look up the definitions of your key words in an online dictionary. Take it further and look at synonyms and antonyms. Last of all, look up other verses similar to your life verse.[1] You're guaranteed a prosperous journey.

Thank You, Lord, for impressing this life verse on my spirit. As I dive deeper into the richness of this promise from You, walk me through it. Guide my eyes to see all the trails You want to lead me on. Be my inspiration as I make this time commitment with You. Let this be a journey of awakening down a lighted path You've set before me.

Today I will begin to understand my life verse fully.

Hidden Treasure

But Mary treasured all these things,
pondering them in her heart.
Luke 2:19, NASB

The Word of God, written for us to read, is treasured in our hearts. When Holy Spirit breathes on Scripture, eternal promises become reality. You are very much like Mary. She knew the Scripture promise of Messiah. She heard the words spoken by Gabriel. And on that fateful day, she birthed her Savior. Mary hid these truths as treasures. Before you begin to share with others, spend time pondering like Mary.

Holy Spirit, I marvel at how a Scripture will come to mind during my day or in a conversation. It's as if the Word I've hidden in my heart comes alive in the present. It's active, vibrant, and full of inspiration. You didn't mean for me to be alone in this walk of faith. As I spend quiet time with You, with the Word, and listening to anointed messages, I build up my treasure chest with nuggets I can share with others.

Today I will recall Holy Spirit's hidden
treasure stored for me.

Study Buddy

SEPTEMBER 9

The LORD God said, "It is not good for the man to be alone.
I will make a helper suitable for him."
Genesis 2:18, NIV

Picture a tandem bike built for two. Someone is in the lead, but both pedal. You'll get to where you're going twice as fast, leaning into the curves in unison. Marriage, family, partnership, friendship, and fellowship are in God's heart. He created us for communion not only with Him but with others. This fellowship is especially true when you read and study the Word with someone. Ask the Lord who might be your study buddy.

Lord, I love studying Your Word on my own. The deeper I go, the richer the revelation and inspiration. But, Lord, I don't think You meant me to keep it just for myself. Could You show me one or two friends I can strike up a sharing experience with? Maybe it's an online devotional[1] or sharing and comparing my thoughts about His Word. Show me the best way for me and my buddy.

Today the Lord will highlight a study buddy or two.

Kindred Spirits

For I have no one else *of kindred spirit who*
will genuinely be concerned for your welfare.
Philippians 2:20, NASB

In today's Scripture, Paul wrote to the church about sending Timothy, his spiritual son, to their church. "Kindred" can be translated as like-minded or of the same mind or spirit, but its actual Greek meaning is "equal souled."[1] God created you to link with others in a mutual chain of love and respect. You, what you hold dear, what you think, what moves your heart, and what motivates your spirit are needed for others. It's time to find your kindred spirits to be mentored and to mentor.

I am grateful, Lord, for the spiritual moms and dads You've sent into my life. They have wonderfully impacted my growth. I ask You to bless them for mentoring me. Now, Lord, I believe I'm ready to do the same. Highlight those people in my life who have a kindred spirit. Connect us as only You can, and let us expand to others.

Today I will ask the Lord for kindred spirit opportunities.

Find the Hungry Ones

Jesus said to them, "I am the bread of life;
the one who comes to Me will not be hungry, and the one
who believes in Me will never be thirsty."
John 6:35, NASB

There comes a time when you must follow the leading of Holy Spirit, cut off the unhealthy, and encourage new growth. Others influence your life and especially your worldview. Do your friends or your church increase your hunger and thirst for more? Are you being challenged to deepen your spiritual knowledge, faith, and action?

Jesus, I confess that I am hungry and thirsty for more of You in my life. I don't want to be passive or unresponsive to Your encouragement to go farther with You. I want to grow and impact others' lives by encouraging their hunger and thirst for more. If I need to make any changes, I open myself to You now. Show me, Lord. Lead me according to Your will.

Today I will ask Jesus to increase my hunger
and thirst for more.

You're in His Book

Then those who feared the LORD spoke to one another,
And the LORD listened and heard them; So a book of
remembrance was written before Him For those who fear
the LORD And who meditate on His name.
Malachi 3:16, NKJV

Have you ever sensed the Lord's presence and pleasure when talking to your friends about Him? The energetic light in those conversations is almost tangible. It's meaty. It's inspiring. It's a yes-yes-yes! Faith rises. Conviction stands. Voices praise. How could the Lord not listen and want it recorded in His Book of Remembrance?

I know You are always with me, Lord. I trust and rejoice in that truth. I enjoy being with my Christian friends who love and worship You as I do. It's almost like it's a symphony of wonder that we share. Even if it's only one or a few, we love to talk about You, what we've learned in Your Word, or a deeper revelation of Scripture. It amazes me that you listen in and record it.

Today I will share something special
about God with a friend.

Tried and True Friends

A friend loves at all times, and a brother
is born for a time of adversity.
Proverbs 17:17, NIV

A tried and true friend is someone you trust. They've earned your respect. You know their integrity and trust them to be true to their word. True friendship and even true love aren't proven until put to the test. Just as Jesus laid down His life for you and all mankind, are you willing to go the extra mile? Christlike character in a friend is a treasure beyond measure.

Lord, today I want to pray for my friends. Thank You for the gifts You've given me through my spiritual friends. They bless my life in so many ways. They are Your hands and feet to me. I ask You to increase in their lives. May You shower them with favor in their homes, work, and wherever their hearts lead them. Stay close to them. Protect, guide, and provide for their every need.

Today I ask the Lord to bless my spiritual friends with favor.

Together as One

So continuing daily with one accord in the temple,
and breaking bread from house to house, they ate their
food with gladness and simplicity of heart.
Acts 2:46, NKJV

One hundred twenty disciples waited together for ten days in Jerusalem after Jesus's ascension into heaven. They were in one accord, meaning they were with one mind or with the same faith or passion. Later, we see they were still in one accord as they shared from house to house. Home gatherings, Bible studies, and fellowship are impactful in building a faith community. What about you? If you're not in one, why not join one?

Jesus, before You ascended, You charged Your disciples to take
Your message to Jerusalem, Judea, Samaria, and the ends of the
earth.[1] These were ever-widening circles. Lord, I want to be Your
messenger too. You didn't mean for me to be isolated. Guide me to
a group of believers who will enhance my walk and benefit from my
participation.

Today I will pray about widening my circle of influence.

Journal with Jesus

Let the words of my mouth and the meditation
of my heart Be acceptable in Your sight, O LORD,
my strength and my Redeemer.
Psalm 19:14, NKJV

Psalm 19 is a magnificent journey of revelation and praise for the Lord, ending with the above verse. Like David, you might feel small in comparison to an all-powerful God. How could He even have time for me and my problems? And yet, He can, and He does. Keeping a record of highlighted verses, thoughts, questions, and even your prayers in a journal will bless you. He won't reject your words or meditations. He simply loves time with you.

It feels so good to write my thoughts in a journal, Lord. Whether good or bad, sorrowful or full of praise, keeping a record of our journey together is rewarding. You watch me from beginning to end, but I only see from issue to issue. It's good to look back and see how far I've come because You are so near.

Today I will journal my thoughts about
myself and the Lord.

Record His Whispers

And He who sits on the throne said,
"Behold, I am making all things new." And He said,
"Write, for these words are faithful and true."
Revelation 21:5, NASB

Do you have dreams? Do you hear something when you wake up in the morning? Does something flash through your mind while listening to a worship song? When you think about personal issues, do you have an inspiration? What about when you're praying? These are only a few ways the Lord is trying to get your attention. It may be only a short phrase. It's important. Write it down. He's telling you something.

I am amazed, Lord, when I hear something out of the blue and know it's You. I love it when You interrupt my day with a word, a phrase, or a picture. These special times connect me to You in such a powerful way. I know You are the King of the universe, but when You speak to my heart, I feel like I'm in the center of it.

Today, Lord, let me record something special from You.

Replay and Repeat

SEPTEMBER 17

*Love the Lord your God with all your heart and with
all your soul and with all your strength. These commandments
that I give you today are to be on your hearts.*
Deuteronomy 6:5–6, NIV

In this chapter, Moses encouraged Israel to teach these commandments diligently to their children. He even urged them to write them on the doorposts of their houses and gates.[1] Constantly replay God's laws in your thinking, seeing, and speaking. Embed the words of the Lord forever on your mind and heart. Why? So you don't forget God. He will never forget you!

Lord, it delights me when You highlight a Scripture or phrase that deeply impacts me. It's like You are present in my day and my thoughts. I feel as if You want me to grasp something mysterious, almost as if You are telling me Your secrets. I am privileged, Lord. I do love You, Lord, and I want my heart, soul, and strength to demonstrate that to You today and forever.

**Today I will replay and repeat a special
word the Lord has given me.**

Wisdom Asks

SEPTEMBER 18

The fear of the LORD is the beginning of wisdom,
And the knowledge of the Holy One is understanding.
Proverbs 9:10, NASB

There is a vast difference between being afraid of God and fearing God. This year, you've learned to draw near to Him and, this month, become a star pupil of His Word. There is a next-level experience awaiting you. And that is the reverential fear and awe of a sacred, holy God. Friendship, even partnership with God, is precious, and He wants that as the Father, Savior, and Counselor. But there's more ahead as you move to a higher level of wisdom and operate in it.

Mighty God, I read of Your majesty, power, and strength through Your Word. Moses took off his shoes, Isaiah fell to his face, Peter cried out, and Paul was blinded when he saw Your glory. These men knew and loved You, but everything changed when they saw Your glorious power. I want to encounter You. Teach me the fear of the Lord. I want to know You more.

Today I will pray for an increase in
the fear of the Lord.

Remembering

I will remember the works of the LORD;
Surely I will remember Your wonders of old.
Psalm 77:11, NKJV

One of the benefits of journaling or dating Scriptures in your Bible is in your review. If you take the word "remember" apart, it means re-member, or put back together as a whole.[1] Nothing builds your faith like taking a journey down memory lane with Jesus. You'll begin to see His handprints on many aspects of your life. At the time, you might not have understood the test, trial, or suffering, but in the end, you will always see His finishing work in your life.

How do I love You? Let me count the ways. That's how I feel about You, Lord. As I read through my old journals where I poured my heart out to You, I always find Your solution later in the pages. When a Bible passage pops into my head, I see a date from so long ago. You're still talking to me, Lord. I re-member, and I am so very grateful.

Today I will remember the works and
wonders of the Lord in my life.

A Godly Life

His divine power has given us everything we need
for a godly life through our knowledge of him who
called us by his own glory and goodness.
2 Peter 1:3, NIV

Scripture knowledge, spiritual gifts, life experiences—all of these things prepare us to lead a godly life. Sure, there will be hard days. You can't control everyone else in your life, only yourself. You have free will, and the choice is always yours. The beauty of this walk is the Lord's desire to help you every step of the way. And once there, you become the testimony of His glory and goodness.

Lord, I am awestruck by the work You have accomplished in me.
Looking back at where I began with You, I see many changes. My
heart is softer, my patience is calmer, my compassion for others is
genuine, and so many other transformations. Thank You for
teaching me, guiding me, and calling me to Your heart. I'm ready
for more and to do more.

Today I am preparing for anything and
everything You have for me.

Abiding

SEPTEMBER 21

Remain in Me, and I in you. Just as the branch cannot
bear fruit of itself but must remain in the vine,
so neither can you unless you remain in Me.
John 15:4, NASB

The Last Supper chapters, written by the apostle John, are explosive with revelation.[1] This meal was Jesus's last opportunity to communicate His heart to His disciples. He explained His motivation, purpose, desires for them, and future promises. He began with washing their feet as a servant, gave instruction on how to serve others, and blessed them with the promise of Holy Spirit. As you abide with Him daily, His fruit will grow and bless many.

Jesus, Your words are pure and true. I desire to love as You love.
Help me to see the Father's image in everyone I meet. You are the
only way, the only truth, and the only life for me. May Your peace
rest on me and make me an instrument of that peace to others. I
want to abide in You and bear much fruit.

Today I will abide a little longer in His presence.

My Father

Your kingdom come. Your will be done
On earth as it is in heaven.
Matthew 6:10, NKJV

You are now at the stage where it's time to activate your faith in a new way. You know Your God, His love, and purpose for your life. You know the power of asking in Jesus's name. You know the power of Holy Spirit who has filled you. It's time to step into a whole new activation. No more hiding in the shadows. Stand on your foundation. Speak His truth. And be heard.

Jesus, I see the world around me in chaos. Division and confusion influence so many. My concern is rising for those who haven't heard the good news. You've opened my eyes and ears, transformed my thinking, and expanded my heart. I ask You now to embolden my prayers. Ignite the flame in my heart to agree with You that the Father's will be done in my life, my family, and the lives I influence.

Father God's will shall be done on
earth as it is in heaven.

My Provider

Give us this day our daily bread.
Matthew 6:11, NKJV

Abraham, the father of our faith, gave God the name Yahweh Yireh when He provided a ram as a substitute for Isaac. God provided daily manna when Israel wandered in the desert for forty years. And God provided Jesus as the Lamb of sacrifice for the forgiveness of our sins. He longs to provide whatever you need to accomplish your daily life and divine purpose. His delight is in partnering with you and your prayers for the needs of others.

My Lord, my heart is full when I recall all You have done for me over these years. You've been with me through desperate times and shown me a way through to victory. You've seen my challenges with those I've cared for and continue to care for. You've inspired me and directed me to new pathways. I am in awe of You and Your provision. Your mercy and grace are exorbitant, and I love You for it!

God will provide my every need for today's tasks.

My Forgiver

And forgive us our debts, As we forgive our debtors.
Matthew 6:12, NASB

The word "debts" actually means debts in Greek. But in Aramaic, the language Jesus spoke, it means offense or sin.[1] You've heard the phrase "keep short accounts," which works beautifully with a daily cleansing of any sin. Notice that Jesus assumed that we've already forgiven those who've offended us. As we mature in the Lord, there's almost a second sense when we've stepped out of line, and Holy Spirit alarm bells ring inside.

Lord, I never want to take You and the forgiveness I've received for granted. It cost You Your very life, but it's only a small matter of pride for me to ask forgiveness. Don't ever let me lose sight of Your magnificent gift. You made a pathway open to me. The most excellent show of appreciation I can give You is forgiving others as quickly. Help me to be a restorer like You. I want to be a uniter and not a divider.

I will forgive quickly and completely.

My Deliverer

And lead us not into temptation,
but deliver us from the evil one.
Matthew 6:13, NKJV

Of course, a loving Father would never lead you into temptation, but He gives you the indwelling Holy Spirit to raise red flags when you might yield to it. Through His eternal plan of salvation, His deliverance gives you His authority to stand against the evil one. The more you understand your identity in Christ, the more effective your prayer life will become for yourself and others.

> *I thank You, Father, that You always lead me in righteousness. Your Word encourages me to grasp the wonder of my position in Christ and as Your child. I can stand against evil because Jesus's precious blood protects me. He is constantly interceding for me just as He did for Simon Peter at the Last Supper.[1] What's even more marvelous is the opportunity You give me to stand in the gap and pray for others' deliverance as well.*

The Lord will deliver me and those I pray
for from the evil one.

My Shield

SEPTEMBER 26

For the LORD God is our sun and our shield.
He gives us grace and glory. The LORD will withhold
no good thing from those who do what is right.
Psalm 84:11, NLT

On rainy days, we use an umbrella. On excessive heat days, we use a hat. When trying to walk uprightly in a fallen world, we have the Lord God as our shield! You've been reaffirming your identity as a precious daughter and expanding your horizon. You are no longer a lamb grazing in the field. You are a lioness with knowledge, skills, and gifts that will impact your world. His promised good things in answered prayer come by faith and through experiencing His grace and glory.

What a privilege it is to abide under Your shield, Lord. You protect me from the enemy's fiery darts and guide me through faith in Your Word. I am in awe of the grace You pour into my life. You open my heart to compassion, my eyes to others' needs, and my ears to Your whispers. Thank You for being my shield.

I will remain under the Lord's shield
all the days of my life.

My Rock

Since you are my rock and my fortress,
for the sake of your name lead and guide me.
Psalm 31:3, NIV

The life of King David is an amazing study of faith, fearless courage, and internal strength through decades of trial and suffering. There are several books in the Bible about David, but we find the most poignant descriptions in David's own psalms. So often, we hear his faith-filled cry to the Lord. David's example is your example. Today's Scripture is a perfect pattern. He makes a statement of truth and then states his request. You can too.

Oh Lord, I marvel at the privilege of praying Your words back to You. You always honor Your words and promises. Jesus, You are the solid rock on which I stand. You are the living Word of God, and You fill my spirit with confidence. I magnify Your name above all names, Jesus. Hear my declaration today as You lead and guide me to Your highest purpose for my life.

My faith is rock-solid in Jesus, and He
will direct my steps.

My Lord and My God

Thomas said to him, "My Lord and my God!"
Then Jesus told him, "Because you have seen me,
you have believed; blessed are those who have
not seen and yet have believed."
John 20:28–29, NIV

Blessed are you who have not seen Jesus yet have believed. Has it ever really sunk in that you believe in someone you can't see, feel, or touch? And yet, you *do* believe. There was that one particular day when Holy Spirit removed the veil, the eyes of your heart opened, and you believed. Every time you exercise faith through prayer, you affirm the gift of salvation, your Lord and your God.

You transformed me from a lost sinner to a found believer. I recognize that salvation is only the beginning of my journey with You. I am in the last half of my life and want to make every day count. Guide me in these devotions to hear and obey well. Speak to my heart what's on Yours. Give me grace to honor You as my Lord and my God.

I am blessed because I have believed.

Armor-Bearer

So his armorbearer said to him,
"Do all that is in your heart. Go then;
here I am with you, according to your heart."
1 Samuel 14:7, NKJV

This month, we've been stretching ourselves in our studies, declarations, and partnerships with God and others. Today's Scripture focuses on Jonathan's desire to scout the Philistine army. He asked his armor-bearer if he would face the danger with him. As we can see, he served Jonathan wholeheartedly. Before you launch into a direct assignment from the Lord, serving under someone else in leadership is often a helpful learning curve.

Jesus, You are the head of Your church, and authority flows through You to leadership. I would like to serve in a greater capacity. You know me well. You know my gifts, my nature, and even my secret dreams. Show me someone I can come alongside and serve for a while. Help me to learn from them. Following well is just as important as leading well. Help me to serve wholeheartedly.

I will learn to serve well so I can lead well later.

Right Place and Time

The Spirit told Philip, "Go to that chariot and stay near it."
Then Philip ran up to the chariot and heard the man
reading Isaiah the prophet. "Do you understand what you
are reading?" Philip asked. "How can I," he said,
"unless someone explains it to me?"
Acts 8:29–31, NIV

Acts 8 is a fascinating chapter. It revolves around a deacon named Philip. Because of Saul's persecution, church leadership scattered. Philip went to Samaria, and salvations, signs, wonders, and miracles followed his preaching about Jesus. He even had an angelic encounter that sent him to a road outside Jerusalem and a eunuch from Ethiopia. Opportunity is what you can expect when you're all in at the right place and time.

Lord, these are exciting times when the harvest is number one on Your mind. I want to ask You for opportunities to share Your good news with others. Prepare me for any assignment You have in store for me. I want to be ready, willing, and available for whatever doors You open for me.

**I will be at the right place and time
for the Lord's assignment.**

HOW CAN I
PARTICIPATE
IN THE LORD'S HARVEST?

Seasonal change begins with leaves and temperatures falling. Vines and fields have ripened. It's time to prepare for harvesting and storing for the winter. It's a joyful, labor-intensive time where everyone participates. Farmers ready their machines, tools, and laborers for the ingathering of their harvest. As prayer-sowers, we should begin to see the harvest of our labor of love in prayer and declarations.

You'll start this month by freshening up your spiritual tools and weapons. What better place to start than with your spiritual armor? Next, you'll align with Holy Spirit, who equips you and draws your attention to His potential harvest. As October draws to a close, you'll concentrate on your prodigals and unsaved loved ones. May your heart beat as one with the Lord of the harvest.

Empower Me

I pray that from his glorious, unlimited resources he will
empower you with inner strength through his Spirit.
Ephesians 3:16, NLT

As you begin this harvest month, you must understand one foundational truth: Jesus's immeasurable power dwells within your spirit. You are the Lord's representative on this earth. You are His hands, His feet, and His mouth. As His ambassador of grace, He authorizes and empowers you as His representative, especially concerning awareness of the works of the enemy and the ability to defeat his works in your life and those around you.

Thank You, Jesus, for Your gift of faith. It may have begun as a tiny
seed, but my confidence has grown through these years. I have seen
Your power at work in my life and the life of others. There is
nothing beyond Your reach. Today, I ask for even more increase in
my life. Stir my faith. Help me tap into even more of Your resources
to make my work for Your kingdom's sake effective.

Jesus's empowerment will strengthen me beyond
what I can think or imagine.

Increase My Capacity

And may you have the power to understand,
as all God's people should, how wide, how long,
how high, and how deep his love is.
Ephesians 3:18, NLT

Most of us have heard of the great Welsh Revival in 1904 and its memorable song "Here is Love." It describes the love of God as vast as the ocean and praise for Jesus, who ransomed His life for us. How can you participate as a laborer in the Lord's harvest? First and foremost, you must fully comprehend the depth of His love for you and all mankind.

My Lord, it is almost too wonderful to fully grasp when I think about Your immense love for me. You have opened my eyes to Your beauty, grace, and mercy. Without this knowledge, I couldn't love others as You do. I couldn't have Your compassion for the lost and hurting. I couldn't partner with You in my prayers without this incredible truth. Increase my awareness so that I might overflow that love to others.

My understanding of God's love will
increase and flow to others.

Make Me Even Bolder

*Because of Christ and our faith in him, we can now come
boldly and confidently into God's presence.*
Ephesians 3:12, NLT

Today's technological advances are remarkable. We can plug an address into our smartphones, and someone's voice will direct us from start to finish! Now, take that same analogy and apply it to prayer and intercession. You know in your heart that the Lord wants all His children to come home to Him, to be saved and set free from evil influence. Just like our GPS, the Lord shows us the way of boldness through His Word and the power of His name. The time is now, and the season is here. Be bold.

No more twinkle toes, Lord. I'm ready for army boots. You've shown me the way to Your throne by Your shed blood on the mercy seat. The enemy is defeated, but I must boldly exercise my faith in that truth. Join me today in my prayers of intercession for myself, my family, and issues on my heart.

**By faith, I will approach the throne
of grace with boldness.**

Be Magnified in Me

OCTOBER 4

Now all glory to God, who is able,
through his mighty power at work within us,
to accomplish infinitely more than we might ask or think.
Ephesians 3:20, NLT

Have you considered yourself too small or insignificant to affect change in a world of 8.1 billion? You're not alone. Most of us think, *Who? Me?* Yes! You! The key isn't you. The key is Jesus *in* you! In Colossians 1, Paul wrote that this is a hidden mystery revealed to the saints.[1] When you fully grasp the magnitude of your authority and power, it will blow your mind and expand your prayers.

Lord, You've placed me on this earth, in this location, and at this very age for Your divine purpose. I know You're counting on me to walk the path You've laid before me. I commit to partnering with You with my whole heart, spirit, and soul. I affirm that it's Your power at work within me. May everything I say and do from this point forward bring You glory.

I will magnify the Lord in and through my life.

Know Your Enemy

The thief comes only to steal and kill and destroy;
I have come that they may have life, and have it to the full.
John 10:10, NIV

As you prepare for the harvest, one essential task is knowing your enemy. Jesus made the case very clearly. He is the Good Shepherd and loves His sheep so much that He was willing to lay His life down for them.[1] But the thief, the evil one, will always try to obstruct your relationship with the Lord. Although you don't want to glorify the enemy of your soul, you must understand his ways and listen only to the voice of your Shepherd.

Lord, I depend on Your Word to help me understand the work of the enemy and how he attacks me and those I care about. I will listen carefully to the voice of my Good Shepherd and be sensitive to Your alerts. Keep my eyes and ears open. Show me if I have any open doors where the enemy has a foothold in my life.

I choose life and shut the door to the enemy.

The Unseen Enemy

OCTOBER 6

*For we are not fighting against flesh-and-blood
enemies, but against evil rulers and authorities of the
unseen world, against mighty powers in this dark world,
and against evil spirits in the heavenly places.*
Ephesians 6:12, NLT

We never want to glorify the enemy by giving him more credit than our awesome God or His mighty hosts of angels. However, we must recognize that just as there is an order for evil and darkness, there is a higher order for goodness and light. Paul emphasized the importance of using knowledge, wisdom, and understanding in your prayers and intercession. As you prepare for the harvest, ask for revelation on what may hold your prayer targets captive.

Thank You, Holy Spirit, for Your gift of discernment. I understand that this is a spiritual war. I may see things that hinder my prayers in the natural, but You see the hidden and unseen obstacles. Increase my awareness of what might be lurking beyond the veil. Help me craft effective prayers to defeat the enemy.

I will become wise to the ways of the enemy.

Dressed for Duty

OCTOBER 7

*Put on all of God's armor so that you will be able
to stand firm against all strategies of the devil.*
Ephesians 6:11, NLT

It may come as a surprise to you, but have you ever really looked at this verse? Paul told us our spiritual armor is God's armor! You'll find a reference in Isaiah 59:17 (NKJV): *"For He put on righteousness as a breastplate, And a helmet of salvation on His head; He put on the garments of vengeance for clothing, And was clad with zeal as a cloak."* When you put on God's armor, you are fully protected and armed for a winning battle.

I love how You prepare me for battle, Lord. I am merely human, but You have given me the power of Your name, the protection of Your blood, and the indwelling presence of Holy Spirit. On top of all that, You've given me the promises of Your Word and Your own armor. How can I not succeed?

**I will stand firm against the enemy when
dressed in God's armor.**

My Belt of Truth

*Stand firm then, with the belt of truth
buckled around your waist.*
Ephesians 6:14, NIV

Have you ever noticed that weight-lifters wear a heavy leather belt around their waist? It reduces stress on the lower back and stabilizes the spine when lifting. The other advantage of wearing this belt is to strengthen the core. Another way of looking at your belt of truth is to keep you in alignment on the straight and narrow path. Spend some time today thinking about the spiritual truths that strengthen your courage and faith.

I rejoice when I consider the truths of Your Word, Lord. From Genesis to Revelation, I read of Your love for Your creation, desire for relationship, and plans to prosper us through understanding and applying Your truth to our lives. You've given me the greatest weapon, for Your Word is true, and that undermines the great deceiver and liar. As I prepare for the harvest, increase my knowledge of Your truth.

**My belt of truth is strong and keeps
me stable and secure.**

My Breastplate of Righteousness

OCTOBER 9

Stand firm then, with the belt of truth buckled
around your waist, with the breastplate
of righteousness in place.
Ephesians 6:14, NIV

Ancient soldiers wore breastplates. Today's modern soldier wears a flak jacket to protect vital organs against projectiles. As a spiritual warrior, your breastplate of righteousness comes as a result of your faith in the righteousness of Jesus Christ, your Savior. This gift allows you to repel the accusations and lies of the enemy and protects against deception. As you prepare for the harvest, your tender heart needs this safeguard.

Lord, I am forever grateful for Your gift of righteousness. Your covering protects my heart. I know You are constantly interceding for me. I recognize the power of Your name and righteousness in all situations. The enemy might want to attack me because of my sinful nature, but You set me free. I can't earn my righteousness, because it's free. Thank You for this protection as I prepare for the harvest.

I wear the breastplate of righteousness
to protect me from evil.

My Peace Boots

And with your feet fitted with the readiness
that comes from the gospel of peace.
Ephesians 6:15, NIV

We love shoes for comfort, style, and use. But when it comes to spiritual warfare, we need boots! Paul emphasized readiness, which implies careful preparation. Soldiers have three general orders: (1) guard your post until relieved, (2) obey all orders and perform all duties, and (3) report any violations and sound the alarm.[1] Like any good soldier in the King's army, you must be ready to share the gospel of peace at any opportunity. An added benefit is the peace of God that protects against the enemy's assaults.

No matter what the occasion calls for, I am grateful for Your peace that passes understanding. I always sense Your peace in quiet mornings or my busy workday. Help me to be alert to opportunities to share Your good news with others. I want to be ready to switch my shoes to boots at a moment's notice and ask You to keep me prepared with Your peace.

I will have my boots on whenever opportunities arise.

My Shield of Faith

OCTOBER 11

In addition to all this, take up the shield of faith,
with which you can extinguish all
the flaming arrows of the evil one.
Ephesians 6:16, NIV

As children, we responded to name-calling with, "Sticks and stones may hurt my bones, but words can never harm me." The truth of the matter is words can and do hurt. Your enemy knows this and sends a constant barrage. The goal is to cause you to doubt your true identity. Notice that Paul said your shield will extinguish these fiery darts, not just repel or prevent them from hitting you. So, by faith, pick up your shield and advance to the battle.

You teach me so much, Lord, as I read and apply the principles of Your Word. Year after year, I'm growing more assertive in my faith as I recognize the enemy's attacks. When he comes at me or uses others, I'm learning to fight back with the knowledge of who I am in You. Doubt, fear, and anxiety have no place in me when I use my shield.

My shield of faith is polished and always ready for use.

My Helmet of Salvation

OCTOBER 12

Take the helmet of salvation.
Ephesians 6:17, NIV

Your armor is almost complete. The final piece of your safety gear is your helmet. It protects your brain, eyes, ears, and neck. For a believer, where do you think the most significant battle exists? Correct. It's in your mind. But we have the mind of Christ! Salvation also gives you spiritual eyes to see beyond the natural, ears to hear what the Spirit is saying, and a stiff neck and spine to keep you aligned with heaven by faith. Notice that Paul said, "Take." It's a choice you need to make.

Lord, I am so grateful for Your gift of armor, but most especially for my helmet of salvation. Without it, I would be at the mercy of a fallen world, open to deception and lost without hope. I am a blood-washed, forgiven, and equipped soldier of Christ. You've promised me eternity and outfitted me in the finest armor to join the battle with You and Your saints until I get there.

I will take my helmet of salvation and put it on daily.

My Sword of the Spirit

OCTOBER 13

Take the helmet of salvation and the sword
of the Spirit, which is the word of God.
Ephesians 6:17, NIV

No one's spiritual armor is complete without the sword of the Spirit. You've been equipping yourself with the Word of God these last ten months through your declarations. You've learned the power of praying the Scriptures back to the Lord. Just as the Lord formed this world with His spoken words, He's given you the same authority. Protected by His truth, righteousness, peace, faith, and salvation, the Lord now gives you His Word to go on the offense.

Jesus, I am ready to join You in this battle for heaven on earth. I, too, want to see our Father's will done in my life and those lives I can touch through prayer. As I read the Word, Holy Spirit, open my understanding and help me grasp Your Word's hidden truths. Help me to comprehend its mysteries. Sharpen my skills, and sharpen the blade of my sword.

I will take up the sword of the Spirit
daily and use it wisely.

Alert and Persistent

OCTOBER 14

Pray in the Spirit at all times and on every occasion.
Stay alert and be persistent in your prayers
for all believers everywhere.
Ephesians 6:18, NLT

Paul ended his teaching about spiritual armor with a charge to live a life of prayer. With a busy schedule and your to-dos, the needs of others, and unexpected emergencies, it might seem unachievable. That's not the case. Everything emanates from relationship when the Lord is your central focus. He is concerned with what concerns you.

Living a life of prayer is delightful to me, Lord. I love getting dressed with You each morning as I ponder the day ahead. Recounting Your blessings and thanking You for headway on issues near and dear to my heart reminds me of Your interest in everything about me and my life. Even more than that, being able to pray about world and local events and the needs of my family, friends, and church touches my heart with gratitude that You're all ears.

Answered prayers will be my reward when
I am alert and persistent.

Lord of the Harvest

*Then He said to His disciples, "The harvest is plentiful,
but the workers are few. Therefore beseech the Lord
of the harvest to send out workers into His harvest."*
Matthew 9:37–38, NASB 1995

"Beseech" is an unusual word. The Greek word means having a deep, personal felt need or desire.[1] You can read the longing in Jesus when He encouraged His disciples to pray for harvest workers. That's where you come in. Your prayers are sweet incense to the Lord. His love is so great for His children who are far from Him. His ears are always open to the willing, the compassionate, and the committed.

Father, my heart grieves for so many lost in this world. Many have never heard the good news. Others have listened to the gospel, but it landed on stony hearts. Your Spirit draws us to the saving knowledge of Jesus Christ. Hear my plea for the lost today. Pour out Your Spirit. Awaken my heart to what's on Your heart. Cause me to carry this burden to heaven's throne.

**The Lord of the harvest will send His
workers into His harvest.**

Wait for Holy Spirit

OCTOBER 16

*But you will receive power when the Holy Spirit comes
upon you. And you will be my witnesses, telling people
about me everywhere—in Jerusalem, throughout
Judea, in Samaria, and to the ends of the earth.*
Acts 1:8, NLT

On the day Jesus ascended to heaven, He charged the five hundred
who were present to wait in Jerusalem for Holy Spirit to fill them
with power.[1] We know that ten days later, on Pentecost, Holy Spirit
fell upon the 120 who remained together to pray in one accord.
What happened to the other 380 who had seen the risen Christ,
heard His promise, and received His charge to wait in Jerusalem?

*Count me in with the remnant who remained, prayed, and waited,
Lord. Although I may be able to share my testimony and witness
Your work in my personal life, I need the empowerment of Holy
Spirit to be a light to many. I will seek You daily and await insight,
revelation, and understanding. Show me how to pray for those
close to my heart who need salvation.*

Holy Spirit will empower me to be a witness to many.

Pour Out Your Spirit

OCTOBER 17

"In the last days," God says, "I will pour out my Spirit upon all people. Your sons and daughters will prophesy. Your young men will see visions, and your old men will dream dreams."
Acts 2:17, NLT

The church of Jesus Christ was birthed on Pentecost over two thousand years ago. Holy Spirit fulfilled the promise given to prophet Joel in the ninth century BC. The 120 received empowerment from Holy Spirit. But that was only a taste of what is still to come. You are here on the earth now, and this incredible outpouring is still on the horizon.

Lord, I believe the greatest harvest of souls is still ahead. I've seen small revivals over my lifetime, but I expect what's coming will be a record-breaker. Today's culture is so dark, and the darkness will challenge the generations following me. I ask You to pour out Your Spirit on all Your children. Awaken them to Your love and their need for salvation. Cause intercession to rise in Your church and repentance to fall on the lost.

**I will pray and live to see the promised
outpouring of Holy Spirit.**

Prepare in the Spirit

OCTOBER 18

As the Scriptures say, "God has put them into a deep sleep.
To this day he has shut their eyes so they do not see,
and closed their ears so they do not hear."
Romans 11:8, NLT

Paul quoted a Scripture from Deuteronomy where Israel had fallen into idolatry.[1] Blindness, deafness, and hard-heartedness result from a spirit, soul, and mind that haven't awakened to the love of God and the need for a Savior. As a laborer in the Lord's harvest, your effectiveness is based on open eyes to the Spirit, ears to hear His counsel, and a heart for the lost. Harvest begins in your prayer closet.

Lord, today I am seeking inspiration on how to partner with You. I need Your Spirit of revelation to pave the way for my prayers. I want to pray targeted prayers for my loved ones, neighbors, and coworkers. Open my eyes to see their pain, their trauma, and even their wrong thinking. I ask You to give me Your heart for these lost ones.

My eyes, ears, and heart will be open
to Holy Spirit's revelation.

Activate My Faith

And whatever things you ask in prayer,
believing, you will receive.
Matthew 21:22, NKJV

As a student of the Word, you know the heart of the Father for His children. His goodness and mercy long to bring His children home to a restored relationship with Him. That's the very place to begin as you partner with Holy Spirit in this harvest. Ask Him to give you a picture of what that salvation would look like. Stir your heart, and speak it out like it's already happened.

Father, I need a faith picture of what salvation would look like for those I pray for. I know You are with me in this endeavor. Show me what a restored life could look like. Give me the confidence I need to declare it. Sear my heart with a passion that mirrors Yours. Breathe Your power into my prayers of agreement, and let me see Your kingdom come to the lost and hurting.

As I begin to pray for the lost, my faith
will rise to a new level.

Use Your Authority

*Truly I say to you, whatever you bind on earth shall
have been bound in heaven; and whatever you loose
on earth shall have been loosed in heaven.*
Matthew 18:18, NASB

As an ambassador in the kingdom of heaven, Jesus gave you His delegated authority to stand in the gap for those you pray for. You may know of past and current issues like addiction, deception, wounds, trauma, or bad choices. There are many examples in the Word of someone interceding for the sinner, pleading for mercy and moving God's heart on their behalf. So, bind the enemy from interfering, and loose His angels to battle with you.

Lord, I ask You to expose anything obstructing the truth of Your love and mercy from touching hearts. I stand in the gap and bind the enemy of confusion, accusation, and trauma. I plead Your blood over all hindrances and shut the door on the enemy's influence. I call upon Holy Spirit to intervene on their behalf. Surround them with angelic help, and prepare their hearts for the good news.

**I will bind the enemy and loose
heaven's help for the lost.**

Praying Prodigals Home

OCTOBER 21

MY HARVEST PRAYER

Jesus, You promised us that when Holy Spirit comes, He will guide us into all truth. We know that no one can come to You unless the Father, who sent You, draws them. Jesus, You are the Way, the Truth, and the Life.

Therefore, I ask You to open _____'s eyes to see, ears to hear, and heart to understand Your great love for them. May they grasp how wide, how long, how high, and how deep Your love is and that whoever believes in You shall not perish but have eternal life.

Prepare _____'s heart. Draw them to You, and give them dreams. Cause them to have divine appointments. Make Yourself known to them. May Your kingdom come near them, heal their souls, revive their spirits, and awaken them to the power of Your gospel of love.

Use me to stand in the gap for them. Give me words of life to share with them. You hear my fervent prayer, and You will answer it. Based on the Word of God, I ask this in the name of Jesus, who is the Word made flesh. Amen. [1]

A Lamb for a Household

Tell the whole community of Israel that on the tenth
day of this month each man is to take a lamb for
his family, one for each household.
Exodus 12:3, NIV

Have you ever considered your divine purpose in your family? Some families share a heritage of faith, but others do not. Frequently, the Lord anoints one believer in a household, who becomes the sacrificial lamb for the whole family. They carry His heart's burden for the salvation of their souls. We see this principle in Exodus when Israel placed the lamb's blood over the lintel and doorposts. Your prayers accomplish this very protection.

Lord, there are days when I feel like I'm the only one in the battle for the souls of my loved ones, neighbors, and coworkers. But I know You are always with me and battle alongside me. Hear my prayers today for Your abundant life to reach these lost ones. I plead Your precious blood over their lives and ask for a breakthrough.

I will gladly serve as the sacrificial
lamb for my household.

You Carry His Message

"I will send my messenger, who will prepare the way before me.
Then suddenly the Lord you are seeking will come
to his temple; the messenger of the covenant,
whom you desire, will come," says the LORD Almighty.
Malachi 3:1, NIV

Don't ever discount the power of your words and the effect of your testimony. Every transformed life brings glory to Jesus. The light that you carry reflects in your words and actions. The gentleness of your manner, the joy of your expression, and the heart of service you demonstrate to others is a flashing billboard to the power of a godly relationship. You can be the key to the open door of salvation.

I want everyone to know You, Lord, like I do. You fill my heart with joy. You direct my steps with favor and blessing. I embrace this covenant of grace and want others to know it too. Give me the message to speak. Show me how I can demonstrate Your love in a profound way. Make me Your messenger of peace.

My testimony of the Lord's goodness
will prepare His way.

Rejoice with Heaven

OCTOBER 24

Or suppose a woman has ten silver coins and loses one.
Won't she light a lamp and sweep the entire house
and search carefully until she finds it? And when she finds it,
she will call in her friends and neighbors and say,
"Rejoice with me because I have found my lost coin."
In the same way, there is joy in the presence of God's
angels when even one sinner repents.
Luke 15:8–10, NLT

This parable that Jesus shared highlights heaven's overarching passion for the sinner who discovers the way, the truth, and the life and repents. You are not alone in your desire to see souls saved. Heaven is watching and waiting to rejoice with you over your harvest.

Lord, I understand that there is a battle for the soul of the lost. The battle rages not only in the individual's spirit and soul but also in the unseen realm. Send Your angels into this spiritual war. Release them to fight demonic influence, and set up divine encounters so these dear ones find You.

I will rejoice with heaven over His harvest.

Make Me Your Gardener

*The one who plants and the one who waters
have one purpose, and they will each be rewarded
according to their labor. For we are co-workers
in God's service; you are God's field, God's building.*
1 Corinthians 3:8–9, NIV

We are not alone in laboring for God's harvest. All of heaven is rooting for you as you carry Jesus's message of redemption and eternal life. Holy Spirit empowers you with wisdom, revelation, and understanding. The Father destined you to be a cultivator of life. Do your part in His garden that He's called you to tend, and He'll provide you with seed, soil, sun, and water to reap His harvest.

Working alongside You to tend Your garden is a joy, Lord. Thank You for the energy and inspiration to plant, till, care for, and reap a harvest with You. Use me however You wish. I'm willing to take the lead or follow Your harvesters. I just ask that You use whatever I can give to the work You've called me to.

I will be a willing gardener for the Lord.

Give Me Wise Words

OCTOBER 26

Peter's words pierced their hearts, and they said to him
and to the other apostles, "Brothers, what should we do?"
Acts 2:37, NLT

The most significant partner we have for harvesting souls is Holy Spirit. As wisdom personified, He has the words that go straight to the heart of those we share the gospel with. He knows each of us intimately. He knows hidden weaknesses and strengths. He knows past traumas. He knows the hindrances that blind eyes, stop up ears, and close hearts. He especially knows your heart to see them saved and set free.

Holy Spirit, I am confident in You and Your work in my life and the lives of those with whom I share my testimony. Give me Your wisdom and timing as I step out to share the good news with others. Make me bold and fill me with faith and confidence in what I share. I particularly ask for Your timing. Only You know when it's the right time and place for the message You will give me.

I will have wise words to share at
the right time and place.

Faith It Out and Up

And without faith it is impossible to please God,
because anyone who comes to him must believe that he
exists and that he rewards those who earnestly seek him.
Hebrews 11:6, NIV

Nothing is more delightful to Father God's ears than hearing your plea for one of His children. It begins with you and your relationship with Him. It is His joy to answer your faith-filled prayers. The fact that you sacrifice your time, energy, and focus on someone else's need surely touches His desire to bring all of heaven into agreement.

Let my faith soar to its highest level today, Father, as I bring these
names to You. Hear my heart's cry for their salvation. I long to see
them in Your kingdom and their names registered in heaven's Book
of Life. Use my prayers to pull eternity's promise into their souls as
I lift them before Your throne. I plead the precious blood of Jesus
over them and call upon the name above all names, Jesus Christ, to
become their Lord and Savior.

**I will witness the salvation of many through
my faith-filled prayers.**

I Will Not Doubt

And Jesus answered and said to them, "Truly I say to you,
if you have faith and do not doubt, you will not only
do what was done *to the fig tree, but even if you say to this*
mountain, 'Be taken up and cast into the sea,'
it will happen. And whatever you ask in prayer,
believing, you will receive it all."
Matthew 21:21–22, NASB

Whatever we think might be impossible is always possible for our mighty God. One of the most critical aspects of praying harvest prayers is your faith. There cannot be any lingering doubt or twinge of unbelief. If the Lord has put someone on your heart to pray into His kingdom, it's a sure thing.

Lord, nothing is impossible for You. You said it, I say it, and I believe it. I know You always hear my prayers. You know my thoughts and secrets. I also believe You know everything about those I bring to Your remembrance. So, today, hear my prayer for their salvation. Bring them home to You.

The Lord will answer my believing prayers.

He Is Faithful

LORD, you are my God; I will exalt you and praise
your name, for in perfect faithfulness you have
done wonderful things, things planned long ago.
Isaiah 25:1, NIV

Our God lives outside of time. He is without beginning or end but interacts with us in our time. The Lord knows the end from the beginning.[1] He knows whose names are in the Book of Life. Your name is in that book. Who is to say that you are not the key ingredient, the last piece of the puzzle, the final push to secure salvation for your loved one, friend, neighbor, or coworker? Be filled with faith to pray as He is faithful to answer.

Lord, I know that You desire that all your children dwell with You
in eternity. You've placed me here and now in this location on earth
for a purpose. You've made plans for me and for those I pray for.
Receive my worship today for all You have done in my life. May
Your grace and favor rest on me as I join You in this harvest.

The Lord is faithful, and I will be too.

A New Song

He put a new song in my mouth, a hymn of praise
to our God. Many will see and fear the LORD
and put their trust in him.
Psalm 40:3, NIV

You have no idea how important you are to the kingdom of heaven's plans. The life you carry, the light you shine, and the song of praise you sing make a difference in so many lives. You may think, *What difference can I make?* More than you can imagine! Every prayer, every encouragement, every kindness you extend to another is immeasurable. You are an epistle read by many![1]

Lord, make me a vessel of Your glory. Let my joy bubble up and explode in praise. I want to be a witness to the world around me of Your love, compassion, and mercy. Our world is desperate for You. May my song be sweet to Your ears. May my prayers move Your heart of compassion. May my reverence for You impact the lives of many. Use me in any way You like for a great harvest of souls.

Many will hear my song of praise and
put their trust in Him.

Ripe for Harvest

OCTOBER 31

Behold, I tell you, raise your eyes and observe the fields,
that they are white for harvest. Already the one who reaps
is receiving wages and is gathering fruit for eternal life, so
that the one who sows and the one who reaps may rejoice together.
John 4:35–36, NASB

Imagine standing in the throne room of heaven, listening to the Holy Trinity. What would be the number one topic of their discussion? Yes, it would be the promised great harvest of souls. Many prophets have said it will be more than a billion souls. Our expectations are high. How could it get any darker? How long do we have to wait for the outpouring of Holy Spirit?

Jesus, You counseled Your disciples to look up and see the potential for harvest. Open my eyes to see the possibilities around me. Show me how to sow life. Give me opportune moments to share the gospel and my testimony. Just as You have prepared the harvest, help me to see my place as a sower and reaper.

The harvest is ripe, and I will be a willing laborer.

HOW CAN I
EXPRESS MY GRATITUDE?

The cold of winter begins to set in this month. Our wardrobes change to sweaters and boots, and our beds need an extra blanket. We light our fireplaces, bundle up, and seek warmth and coziness. Turning the calendar reminds us of upcoming holidays and family and friend gatherings. It's a perfect time to express gratitude to all who bless you, especially through remembering them in your prayers and declarations.

The first Tuesday in November is reserved for our United States elections. It's a time when every prayer warrior is engaged in prayer and intercession for godly representatives in all levels of government. We appeal to heaven for righteousness in our elected officials. Thankfulness is a powerful weapon, along with prayers, declarations, decrees, praise, and worship.

In keeping with an emphasis on thanksgiving and blessing, the weeks ahead will focus on righteous local, state, and federal elections, our God for His many blessings, our family and friends, our mentors and spiritual leaders, and the generations we serve.

Founding Fathers

NOVEMBER 1

*God, we have heard with our ears, Our fathers have told us
The work that You did in their days, In the days of old.*
Psalm 44:1, NASB

As Americans, we are the most fortunate citizens. Of all the nations on the earth, our Declaration of Independence and Constitution, with its amendments, echo divine truths. Our forefathers were godly men, students of the Word of God, and crafters of our founding documents. For hundreds of years, generations have benefited from their relationship with God. Wisdom flowed from heaven, through them, and now to us.

Lord, I give thanks for the godly men and women You chose to serve our nation at its founding. Their knowledge and worship of You paved the way for generation after generation. Anoint new leaders today to carry the torch of freedom, equality, and brotherhood. Help me see opportunities to strengthen the heritage I've received and pass it on to future generations.

**Thank You, Lord, for my forefathers and for
establishing leaders of quality.**

Citizens of Heaven

NOVEMBER 2

Above all, you must live as citizens of heaven, conducting
yourselves in a manner worthy of the Good News about
Christ ... standing together with one spirit and one purpose,
fighting together for the faith, which is the Good News.
Philippians 1:27, NLT

We are responsible for living righteously in our nation. Paul wrote that our citizenship in heaven as believers takes precedence. We recognize the importance of respecting authority and obeying the laws of our land to the best of our abilities. Your greatest gift to your neighborhood, city, and state is exercising your responsibilities as a citizen with moral character and integrity, according to the good news.

Thank You, Lord, for establishing truth, justice, and purpose in my
life. I am here, in this city and state, for Your purpose. Guide me in
Your ways to promote unity, respect, and honor for all those in
government. May my words and actions reflect those of Yours in
heaven as I represent You here on earth.

Thank You, Lord, for Your wisdom to live as
a good citizen of heaven and earth.

Accountability in Authority

Have confidence in your leaders and submit
to their authority, because they keep watch over you
as those who must give an account.
Hebrews 13:17, NIV

As mature Christians, we must vote to elect godly officials in all categories. From local judges, school board directors, mayors, and city council members up to county, state, and federal elections, we vote for those we feel will best serve us and our communities. More than any time in our history, it is crucial that godly citizens seek the best and brightest to lead and govern. May they administrate with the knowledge and fear of the Lord as they will give an account.

Father, thank You for the callings and gifts You've given to those
who serve our communities in governmental offices. Cause the best
and brightest among us to heed Your call to service. Give them
favor with the electorate. Call the Deborahs, Miriams, Josephs,
and Daniels, and anoint them for positions of authority. Help them
to understand and honor their responsibilities.

Thank You, Lord, for those who have answered
the call to serve in office.

Wise Leaders

NOVEMBER 4

When there is moral rot within
a nation, its government topples easily.
But wise and knowledgeable leaders bring stability.
Proverbs 28:2, NLT

We can never underestimate the power of prayer for those who lead us. During these past decades, we've seen the rise of evil ideologies and the fall of godly principles. Our courts have ruled against prayer, the life of the unborn, and the sanctity of marriage. Crime and violence fill our city streets. But God! Your prayers do have an impact. How? Your prayers agree with God's ultimate authority. When we pray according to God's will, we know He hears and answers us.[1]

Lord, I recognize that I play an integral part in establishing a godly government. I will exercise my duty to vote for wise and knowledgeable leaders. And I will pray daily, especially during the election week, for fair and honest elections. I know You hear the cry of my heart for Your hand to be upon those in leadership. Let heaven's will be done in my city, state, and nation.

Thank You, Lord, for establishing wise and knowledgeable leaders in government.

Reveal Their Hearts

NOVEMBER 5

They all prayed, "Lord Yahweh, you know the heart
of every man. Please give us clear revelation
to know which of these two men you have chosen."
Acts 1:24, TPT

In the Old Testament, the Lord gave the high priest the Urim and Thummim, which were gemstones he carried in his breastplate or ephod. When the people had a question for the Lord, they would call for the high priest, and the stones would answer. Later, Israel sought a prophet. Just as the first apostles in their day, you have Holy Spirit to guide you. Pray. Ask for wisdom. Do your research. Vote with peace.

I thank You, Lord, that You desire for us to have godly servants in
government. Help us to see through the smoke and mirrors. Cause
their characters to be exposed. Let their words speak truth so that
my decisions align with Your choices. I will do my due diligence,
but I ask for Your guidance. Lead me by Your truth with every
selection.

Thank You, Lord, that You know man's heart
and will indicate Your choice.

Use Discernment

If you are wise, your wisdom will reward you;
if you are a mocker, you alone will suffer.
Proverbs 9:12, NIV

Today's social media world greatly influences our decisions. Promoters of both good and evil spend millions to sway opinion. Sometimes, it's hard to decide who to believe. Sound bites, twisted words, false information, and hostile ideologies compete for your vote. Some citizens are so confused that they skip voting altogether, thinking, *I'm just one vote.* You *do* count, and so does your vote. Exercise your right, and vote with Holy Spirit discernment when you cast your ballot.

Lord, taking a stand for righteousness in leadership is a privilege. I ask for Your wisdom and discernment as I read the flyers, listen to the news, hear debates, and scan social media. Give me the insight I need to listen and read between the lines. Lead me to trusted people, whose opinions I can depend on, and give me Your heart for these candidates.

**Thank You, Lord, for trusting me to
make the right decisions.**

For the Children's Sake

NOVEMBER 7

*Tell it to your children, and let
your children tell it to their children,
and their children to the next generation.*
Joel 1:3, NIV

Let's return to the central premise as we close our election
devotions this week. God has given you dominion over the earth.
He trusts you to know His will and desires you to exercise that
authority. He is sovereign, yet He's given you the power to choose.
What you do impacts the lives of your children and grandchildren,
even the generations that follow. Elections matter. Your vote is your
stamp of approval and sets the stage for the next generation. Vote
wisely, and encourage others of like mind to do so as well.

*Father, You rule the heavens, but the earth You've given to man.[1] I
am concerned for myself and future generations. Cause righteous
men and women to want to serve in my city, state, and nation's
government. Bring them the finances and staff to help them run
campaigns with integrity. May they find favor in Your sight.*

**Thank You, Lord, for securing future generations
with excellent government.**

Thank You, Yahweh-Roi

NOVEMBER 8

She gave this name to the LORD who spoke to her:
"You are the God who sees me," for she said,
"I have now seen the One who sees me."
Genesis 16:13, NIV

Imagine you are the slave, Hagar, who conceived a son for Abram. You got a little too big for your shoes, but being cast out seems extreme. The angel of the Lord met her and gave her advice and a promise. She returned with a new attitude and later gave birth to a son. Sometimes, correction may seem harsh, but gratitude flows when wisdom and answers come forth. Yahweh-Roi sees your deepest needs and will always lead you on the right path.

You are the God who sees me. You've always seen me—from growing in my mother's womb to my birth, to my first steps, and to today. I am never out of Your sight. You see me when I slip and fall. You watch over me in my struggles as well as my victories. I choose to abide under Your shadow forever.

Thank You, Yahweh-Roi, for seeing me.

Thank You, Yahweh-Yireh

NOVEMBER 9

Abraham named the place Yahweh-Yireh
(which means "the LORD will provide").
To this day, people still use that name as a proverb:
"On the mountain of the LORD it will be provided."
Genesis 22:14, NLT

Perhaps the greatest test of Abraham's faith was the demanded sacrifice of his son, Isaac. Abraham's message to the servants accompanying them to Mount Moriah is sometimes missed. He told them they were going to worship but would return.[1] Obedience is where the rubber meets the road. You know God's character. He is good, kind, loving, and always wants what's best for you. God called Abraham to make a sacrifice, but God provided the ram. Trust Him to provide His best for you too.

I am amazed, Lord, when I think of all the ways You provide for me. First and foremost, through Jesus's sacrifice, I have access to heaven's throne. My faith assures me that all I need is in and through You. And best of all, I believe that where You guide, You always provide.

Thank You, Yahweh-Yireh, for providing everything I need.

Thank You, Yahweh-Shalom

NOVEMBER 10

And Gideon built an altar to the LORD there
and named it Yahweh-Shalom
(which means "the LORD is peace").
Judges 6:24, NLT

When the Lord appeared to Gideon to call him to champion the fight against the Midianites, he doubted and tested the angel of the Lord. When he realized it was the Lord, he cried out in great fear because he'd seen the Lord face-to-face. The Lord reassured him, and Gideon built an altar of worship to acknowledge God's peace.[1] In the deepest, darkest of times, when doubt rises up, there is only one solution for you: call upon the Lord, who is peace.

Lord, there is so much meaning in Your name, Yahweh-Shalom. It is more than just calm and rest. To me, it means You make me whole again. You bring wisdom and order to the disorder in my life. I'm able to make well-reasoned decisions because I experience Your peace. You are perfection, and You complete me.

Thank You, Yahweh-Shalom, for being my peace.

Thank You, Yahweh-Nissi

Moses built an altar there and named it Yahweh-Nissi
(which means "the LORD is my banner").
Exodus 17:15, NLT

Moses commanded Joshua to battle the Amalekites. Moses climbed a hill and watched Joshua in the valley. As long as Moses's hands were lifted in prayer, Joshua succeeded. When he tired and lowered his hands, Israel lost ground. Aaron and Hur then sat Moses down, held up his hands, and the battle was won. Just like Moses, you honor the Lord when you affirm His rule, His righteousness, and His call upon your life. And sometimes, He covers us with others He sent to our aid.

Lord, I always want to remember how You cover me with Your protection. You are my banner, the flag I stake in the ground that says, "My God will fight my battles for me." The battle always belongs to You. My job is to trust, obey, and fulfill my part of the covenant. With my hands lifted high, I will always praise and thank You.

Thank You, Yahweh-Nissi, for covering me
with Your might and mercy.

Thank You, Yahweh-Rapha

NOVEMBER 12

If you will listen carefully to the voice of the LORD
your God and do what is right in his sight, obeying his
commands and keeping all his decrees, then I will not make
you suffer any of the diseases I sent on the Egyptians;
for I am the LORD who heals you.
Exodus 15:26, NLT

The Lord made this covenant agreement with Israel in the wilderness. Israel witnessed all ten plagues in Egypt, but only three affected them. The Lord's hand of protection was upon them. You serve a mighty God of miracles who desires to protect, shield, and heal His children.

Lord, You have no idea how grateful I am that I can present large and small needs to Your attention. You care as much about my hurt feelings and a stubbed toe as a broken leg. What hurts me hurts You. It brings me such comfort to know You hear me, especially when I pray for others' needs. Your heart is always to save, heal, and deliver.

Thank You, Yahweh-Rapha, my God, who
heals my body, spirit, and soul.

Thank You, Yahweh-Chereb

NOVEMBER 13

How blessed you are, O Israel! Who else is like you,
a people saved by the LORD? He is your protecting shield
and your triumphant sword! Your enemies will cringe
before you, and you will stomp on their backs!
Deuteronomy 33:29, NLT

When you have a battle to face, who do you want to lead you? None other than the Lord, the Sword. His Word is alive, active, and more powerful than a two-edged sword.[1] Your most potent weapons are what He's said to you and His promises in His Word. How marvelous is His sword that always leads you in triumph!

When I think of Your words and promises, I just want to jump and shout. I am blessed because You always go before me with Your sword of deliverance. I never have to face a battle alone. You shield me with Your love and power. You lead me into victory. And, Lord, it means so much to me that You battle for those I love too.

Thank You, Yahweh-Chereb, for Your triumphant sword.

Thank You, I AM

NOVEMBER 14

God said to Moses, "I AM WHO I AM."
Exodus 3:14, NIV

Have you ever thought about our God's divine names? The Bible reveals hundreds of titles of God as One, but it also expresses the Father, Son, and Holy Spirit as separate identities. In all cases, these titles reveal His perfect character. One of the most unique names is God's direct response to Moses. It's almost an invitation for you to fill in the blank. Think of it this way: "I am who you need Me to be."

You are my Lord, my Creator, my Peace, my Comforter, my Teacher, my Redeemer, my Lover, my Provider, my Peace, my Banner, my Covering, my Hiding Place, my Strong Tower, my Refuge, my Companion, my Reconciler, my Sword, my Shield, my Shepherd, my Kinsman Redeemer, my Abba, my Betrothed, my Savior, my Righteousness, my Answer, my Master, my Sanctifier, my All-Sufficient One, my Door, my Eternal Promise, my Miracle, my Judge, my Messiah, my Hope, and my Reward. You are my Everything.

**Thank You, I AM, for being You in
all Your expressions.**

Fathers and Mothers

NOVEMBER 15

Honor your father and your mother,
that your days may be long upon the land which
the LORD your God is giving you.
Exodus 20:12, NKJV

Not all of us have had the same experience of being parented. Some of us were wanted, and some were not. Some were abandoned, in foster care, or adopted. You may have had godly parents or never set foot in a church as a family. You may have been an only child or one of many. All of us have a history, whether good or bad. But none of us have an excuse to disregard the Lord's command.

Lord, in a perfect world, I would have perfect parents to love, nurture, and raise me to love, honor, and serve You. Regardless of whether my parents raised me in the admonition of the Lord, I want You to know that I honor You by honoring them. They gave me life and, with that, a destiny and purpose in You and through You.

Thank You, Lord, for my father and mother,
who brought me into Your world.

Brothers and Sisters

Say of your brothers, "My people,"
and of your sisters, "My loved one."
Hosea 2:1, NIV

Whether you come from a large or small family, blood is thicker than water. We recognize birth order as a potent variant in relationships. Talents, giftings, and even gender make a huge difference in your success in life when it comes to family interaction. Think of Joseph's and David's brothers, Miriam, Aaron, and Moses, James and John, or Mary and Martha. Some of these relationships were not so great; others are examples of great partnerships.

Lord, You knew what You were doing when and where You placed me in my family. I trust in Your unfailing love and great wisdom. Help me to be a living example of that love to my brothers and sisters. I ask for patience, compassion, and a generous spirit. Show me ways I can encourage them. Soften my heart over disagreements, and help me to always pursue unity with Your grace.

Thank You, Lord, for my brothers
and sisters. Bless them.

Sisters in Christ

Peter went with them, and when he arrived he was taken upstairs to the room. All the widows stood around him, crying and showing him the robes and other clothing that Dorcas had made while she was still with them.
Acts 9:39, NIV

This story of Tabitha (Dorcas in Greek) is so touching. She was well known in Joppa for helping the poor but fell sick and died. Grief-stricken, the widows sent men to find Peter, who was nearby. Their grief and Peter's faith raised her from the dead. Sisterhood is powerful. You know who you can count on for hearts and hands when needed.

Lord, today I want to thank You for all the lovely women You've placed in my life. They support me when needed, know me like a book, keep me accountable, and encourage my growth and maturity. They laugh with me in joy and cry with me in sadness. They are an extension of You. Help me to be quick to respond to their needs.

**Thank You, Lord, for my sisters
in Christ. Bless them.**

Coworkers

I thought I should send Epaphroditus back to you.
He is a true brother, co-worker, and fellow soldier.
And he was your messenger to help me in my need.
Philippians 2:25, NLT

Can you imagine traveling through this life without helpful, giving, committed coworkers? Whether in ministry or your day job, willing hands that share the same vision to get the job done right can make or break you. Fortunately, you can be the one who fosters productivity and even joy in the workplace. Sharing a vision, pulling out the best, encouraging each other, and celebrating a job well done brings rewards.

Lord, there is no way I could get as much done at work, at church, or even in my home without willing hearts and hands. Thank You for bringing so many wonderful people into my life. Bless them with promotion. And, Lord, for those who just seem to drag us down a bit or don't seem as focused on the job, give me an understanding of their needs. Help me to lift them to a better place.

Thank You, Lord, for my coworkers. Bless them.

Neighbors

NOVEMBER 19

*"And you shall love the Lord your God with
all your heart and with all your soul and
with all your mind and with all your strength."
The second is this: "You shall love your neighbor as yourself."
There is no other commandment greater than these.*
Mark 12:30–31, ESV

A wave is one thing, but redelivering a box or alerting someone about a broken sprinkler is another. An extra loaf of banana bread, retrieving a bounced ball, chicken soup, babysitting, and keeping a clean yard are little ways we appreciate and love our neighbors. The peace of your neighborhood is dependent on a community spirit of respect, honor, and courtesy.

Lord, I thank You for my neighbors. Even though my kids are grown, I love the sound of children's laughter. Bless these families with salvation and purpose. Thank You for their watchful eye on my property. Bless my effort to get to know them. Show me ways I can demonstrate Your love. Answer my prayers for their needs.

Thank You, Lord, for my neighbors. Bless them.

Service Workers

Do you see a person skilled in his work?
He will stand before kings;
He will not stand before obscure people.
Proverbs 22:29, NASB

We're all busy people with plenty on our plates. Everyone is up early to something, whether plumbing, roofing, pool sweeping, housekeeping, baking, slicing, or serving. And then there are cashiers, restockers, dog walkers, salespeople, police, bus drivers, tellers, crossing guards, and so on. Have you ever really noticed how many of us actually spend our lives serving others? The Father does. Jesus does. And Holy Spirit does. Perhaps we should as well.

Lord, I am so grateful to the hundreds of people I see each week as I hurry and scurry to do my errands. Help me remember to wave, smile, or acknowledge them in some special way. Remind me to brighten their days as they ease mine. Thank You for these hardworking people. I'm sure You see them. Let them know that what they do matters to many.

Thank You, Lord, for service workers. Bless them.

Our Life Savers

This is my command—be strong and courageous!
Do not be afraid or discouraged. For the LORD
your God is with you wherever you go.
Joshua 1:9, NLT

Imagine dedicating your life to fighting fires, answering 911 calls, driving an ambulance, investigating crime, restoring peace, protecting lives, or serving in the Armed Forces. In every case, they face danger and must make life-and-death decisions in seconds. We are so fortunate to have men and women who answer the call to serve their communities and nation in this way.

Father, thank You for gifting so many with the skill and fearlessness to face danger so I don't have to. I am grateful for the conquering and compassionate gifts You've deposited in them. Today I lift them before You and ask for Your provision in their lives. Give them excellent commanders, increase the skills and equipment needed, and protect their families as they serve ours.

Thank You, Lord, for the first responders
who save lives. Bless them.

353

The Apostolic Gift

NOVEMBER 22

For we speak as messengers approved by God
to be entrusted with the Good News.
1 Thessalonians 2:4, NLT

One of the most important ministries in equipping the saints for the work of the ministry is the apostolic gift. These men and women are gifted to set the foundation and cast the vision for the rest of us. Consider Abraham, Joseph, Moses, Miriam, Joshua, David, and Deborah. We think of Jesus's disciples and apostles. They literally gave their lives for their assigned work. Think of the leaders you follow today, and then thank God for them!

Lord, You have always raised up generals of the faith to lead us on. It doesn't matter if they were thousands of years or centuries ago. Their messages, writings, and leadership have set Your foundation for many of us. And, Lord, I also want to thank You for the internet that brings today's apostolic messages into my home. I need men and women of vision in my life.

Thank You, Lord, for depositing Your
apostolic gift in today's leadership.

The Prophetic Gift

NOVEMBER 23

For the Lord GOD does nothing without revealing
his secret to his servants the prophets.
Amos 3:7, ESV

Ephesians 2:20 tells us that the church is built upon the foundation of the apostles and prophets, with Jesus Christ as the cornerstone. We need the one who sees and hears the vision and the one who knows how to build it. Holy Spirit not only counsels you as His child, but He also guides your leaders. Jesus warned us to know the prophetic signs and seasons.[1] That means we need to see and hear His voice, be watchful, and be ready to respond.

Lord, I thank You for speaking to me through Your Word and the messages of those You've anointed to know the signs and seasons we live in. Thank You, Lord, for the promise of an outpouring of Your Spirit in glory in the days ahead.[2] I do believe for signs, wonders, and miracles, as well as a glorious harvest of souls, before Your second coming.

Thank You, Lord, for stirring Your prophetic gift in our leaders and me.

355

The Teaching Gift

Let the elders who rule well be considered worthy
of double honor, especially those who labor
in preaching and teaching.
1 Timothy 5:17, ESV

Spiritual mentors, whether from the Bible or through teachings today, expand our knowledge of the Word. They instill a hunger to know more, to glean every nuance or symbolism that shows us the hidden things. You can read the Bible, but you need a skilled teacher to fully appreciate its magnificent truths. They connect the dots and fill us with their faith.

Lord, I can't thank You enough for the men and women who have fed me spiritually. It's as if they started with a baby spoon and ended with a shovel. They opened my mind to more, and I am forever grateful. Not only that, I have today's technology, podcasts, Bible programs, blogs, devotionals, downloadable books, newsletters, email, and video messages. It's mind-boggling. Thank You for these messengers of love, hope, and devotion to You.

Thank You, Lord, for the teachers You've
given me. Bless them doubly.

The Pastoral Gift

NOVEMBER 25

*The Spirit of the Lord GOD is upon Me, Because
the LORD has anointed Me To preach good tidings
to the poor; He has sent Me to heal the brokenhearted,
To proclaim liberty to the captives, And the opening
of the prison to* those who are *bound.*
Isaiah 61:1, NKJV

Jesus proclaimed this verse when He began His ministry on the earth.[1] As our Good Shepherd, He modeled the perfect pastor. He always sought out the lost, the forgotten, the hurting, the shamed, and the sick, leading them to wholeness. How fortunate we are when we are under the watchful eyes of a caring pastor.

Over the years, I have had many pastors, Lord. Each one has deposited something of You into my spiritual life. Thank You for these men and women who have been so unselfish with their time and faith. I ask that You fill them with even more knowledge of You. Meet their personal and family needs. Surround them with strong elders and willing helpers to share the burden of ministry.

**Thank You, Lord, for the pastoral gifts You've
given the church. Bless them.**

The Evangelism Gift

NOVEMBER 26

How, then, can they call on the one they have
not believed in? And how can they believe in the one
of whom they have not heard? And how can they
hear without someone preaching to them?
Romans 10:14, NIV

When you think of an evangelist, what is the first word that comes to mind? Passion? Faith? Exuberance? Boldness? All of those and more, like fire! There's nothing quite like hearing the salvation message from an anointed speaker. They make you want to get saved all over again. But there is another side too. What about the missionary who gives a year or a lifetime to meet the needs of the lost?

Lord, not all of us are bold and courageous. I'm kind of shy, but
You know that. I am thankful that You anoint others to share the
gospel with such passion. Thank You for those You put in my life
with whom I can share my faith. I want everyone to know You as I
do. And, Lord, bless all who serve You in the mission field.

Thank You, Lord, for the evangelists.
Give them open doors. Bless them.

The Serving Gift

But to each one of us grace was given
according to the measure of Christ's gift.
Ephesians 4:7, NKJV

Just think about all the men and women who unselfishly serve the body of Christ Sunday after Sunday and year after year: nursery workers, greeters, ushers, sound people, worship teams and choirs, Sunday school teachers, home group leaders, men's and women's ministries, helps ministries, and so on. They aren't people who seek to build their reputation. They simply want to do their best to serve the Lord.

Lord, thank You for all the hidden ones who serve You and Your children behind the scenes. Help me remember to acknowledge them and let them know I see them. Prompt me to pray for them, for Your favor on their lives and families, and for increased anointing and promotion. And, Lord, as I serve, may Your grace be upon me for greater effectiveness in all I set my heart and hands to do.

Thank You, Lord, for those who serve
in Your kingdom on earth.

The Senior Generation

*They will still bear fruit in old age, they will stay fresh
and green, proclaiming, "The Lord is upright; he is
my Rock, and there is no wickedness in him."*
Psalm 92:14–15, NIV

Whether you've attended church since childhood or only attended in
later life, observing the older generation in prayer and worship
touches the heart. Someday, in the not-so-distant future, they will
hear, "Well done, good and faithful servant." They model
faithfulness, humility, tenderness, and compassion. They've seen it
all and still believe for more. They know the Word, and the Word
knows them.

*Thank You, Lord, for the grandmothers and grandfathers of the
faith. I can see Your life in their wrinkles, tender eyes, and smiling
lips. They know You, and it demonstrates all the possibilities of
destiny in a life well-lived. Thank You for these guardians of the
faith. Thank You for all that they've taught us through the years. Be
kind to them, and meet their needs until eternity becomes their
home.*

Thank You, Lord, for the seniors of faith. Bless them.

The Bridge Generation

NOVEMBER 29

One generation shall praise Your works to another,
And shall declare Your mighty acts.
Psalm 145:4, NKJV

If you're over forty, you understand what being the bridge between the generations means. You are caring for aging parents and raising your children and grandchildren. Your lives are full of activity with a heavy sense of responsibility. You may feel that everyone has high expectations, and perhaps they do. Be assured the Lord is watching, smiling, and rooting for you. You may not receive a lot of thanks for what you do, but He surely thanks you.

Lord, I am grateful for the energy You give me. You know my heart to be the best daughter, mother, and grandmother. I want to participate in a legacy of love. Not everything in my history or even today is perfect, but You are always perfect. I don't know what I would do without Your ever-present wisdom and, yes, compassion. You've taught me to love well. Lead me always with Your grace.

Thank You, Lord, for being the source for
the bridge generation. Bless them.

The Next Generations

NOVEMBER 30

We will not hide these truths from our children;
we will tell the next generation about the glorious deeds
of the LORD, about his power and his mighty wonders.
Psalm 78:4, NLT

You may be a mother, grandmother, or aunt, and you see what we all see: a lost generation with eyes glued to their phones, tattoos, pierced bodies, and punky hair. Our heads shake, and our hearts grieve. Where have we gone wrong? What can we do? You can pray. You can stand. You can vote. You can speak the truth in love. You can encourage. You can model. You can seek the Lord.

Thank You, Lord, that You have given my generation great promises. You said that darkness would fill the earth in the last days, but Your glory would appear over us. You promised an outpouring of Your Spirit on our sons and daughters. You promised that all our sons and daughters will be taught of the Lord, and they would have great peace.[1] I know You keep Your promises. Thank You.

Thank You, Lord, for Your promises to
the next generations. Bless them.

Everyone enjoys this month as we prepare for holiday traditions, family gatherings, social events, gift exchanges, and celebrating our Savior's birth. The season's sights, sounds, and smells emote many memories of the past and warm our hearts. It's our time to give and receive.

If you're like most thoughtful, prayerful women, you also review the year's challenges and victories and consider hope-filled plans for next year. This month's devotionals will encourage you to think beyond today and into your tomorrows.

You'll begin (as you always do) considering others first. Just as children delight in creating their list for Santa, take some time to create your own list for God. Celebrate the Lord's gifts in you and others, and bless them. As the year draws to a close, you will reaffirm the new *me* you've become and make plans to further your growth into the new year and beyond.

The Gift of Beauty

DECEMBER 1

Oh, taste and see that the LORD is good!
Psalm 34:8, ESV

Father God loves to awaken all of your senses to His creation, whether through your surroundings, His creatures, or others. Melodies soothe and enliven you. Aromas arouse you. But the most incredible beauty of all is the inner eye and heart of the beholder. Beauty attracts and arrests your attention. You stop in your tracks, and your heart responds. Ask the Lord to show you His loveliness this holiday season. In particular, ask Him to show you His beauty in those around you.

Lord, in this season of gift-giving and receiving, help me see Your children's beauty. When I look at people at work, in the marketplace, at church, and even in my home, open my eyes to see them as You do. Let me taste and see what You see in them. Use my awareness to draw more of Your Spirit out of them. Give me words of encouragement to lift them up.

**I will see God's beauty in others
this Christmas season.**

The Gift of Delight

DECEMBER 2

Delight yourself also in the LORD,
And He shall give you the desires of your heart.
Psalm 37:4, NKJV

There's nothing more satisfying than finding the perfect gift for a loved one. You know, beyond a doubt, that it's ideal for that person. God created you with the capacity to give and receive pleasure. You know joy because He is joy. Delight is the opposite of being numb to the world, each other, yourself, and the Creator. When you delight in Him and those He created, abundance flows to and through you.

Just as I watch the excited faces of the young when they unwrap their gifts, I can imagine what You must feel seeing my delight when You meet my heart's desires. Do You just smile, or do You let out a belly laugh? Do You jump up and down like me? Do You call the angels to rejoice with You? Somehow, I bet You do. Thank You for being my delight.

I will laugh and clap with delight when
I see You answer prayers.

The Gift of Love

DECEMBER 3

We love, because He first loved us.
1 John 4:19, NASB

Isn't it interesting that you can *love* a particular food, activity, or song all by yourself? To truly experience the gift of love, it takes selfless interaction with another. It begins and ends with an open heart that cherishes the other more than the self. It's *we* and not *me*. Where do you think love began? Was it in Eden with a single breath or in Bethlehem with a baby's first cry? Consider how you might express love to those around you. Be an initiator this holiday season.

Such a small four-letter word, L-O-V-E, but it speaks volumes, Lord. Thank You for loving me and showing me the way of love through Your Word. My Bible has sixty-six books expressing Your loving desires for connection and covenant, but this verse says it all. As I prepare to celebrate Your Son's birth once again, may my heart be overflowing toward You and my world.

Because I am well-loved, I will love well this season.

The Gift of Presence

DECEMBER 4

*And He said, "My Presence will
go with you, and I will give you rest."*
Exodus 33:14, NKJV

If you ask most busy women what they want for Christmas, they'd most likely say, "Me-time." A spa day, an unhurried lunch with a friend, or a checked-off list might also fit the bill. What you have at your disposal twenty-four-seven is the precious presence of the Lord. Grace pours from His throne, but you must put yourself before it. How? Sit quietly, take a few deep breaths, open your hands, and say, "Come, Prince of Peace." He's yours anytime you need Him.

In this place of rest and quiet, Your presence envelopes me. All the weight of the world that I carry on my shoulders, I give over to You as the weight of Your love and glory renews me. Challenges become small, and solutions flow because You care so much about me. As I fix my eyes on You and tune my heart to Yours, I welcome Your presence and rest.

I will rest in the presence of the Lord and be refreshed.

The Gift of Mornings

DECEMBER 5

My voice You shall hear in the morning, O LORD;
In the morning I will direct it to You, And I will look up.
Psalm 5:3, NKJV

Life is just life, complete with storms, challenges, joys, and celebrations. Like everyone, you have good days and bad days. But one thing you have that many don't is your morning with the Lord. No person or situation can take that from you. When the new day dawns, hope surges, possibilities begin to take shape, and light shines in the darkness.

Lord, I cherish my mornings with You. I love focusing on just You and me. Sharing my needs with You, lifting up others in prayer for their needs, and simply listening for Your voice prepares the flow for the rest of my day. I delight in this quiet stillness with You. Thank You for regenerating my focus on You and Your mighty power to change everything. I love being Your daughter, Your partner, and Your friend.

Morning by morning, You are my
favorite part of the day.

The Gift of Encouragement

DECEMBER 6

*And David was greatly distressed, for the people
spoke of stoning him, because all the people were bitter
in soul, each for his sons and daughters. But David
strengthened himself in the LORD his God.*
1 Samuel 30:6, ESV

Sometimes, it's a wink, a nod, a prick, or a prod. Other times, it's a note, a call, a text, a compliment, or even an "I see you." You are no different than everyone else. All thrive when efforts are acknowledged. Encouragement builds hope and strengthens confidence. When no one else is there, the Lord God is!

There is no one like You, Lord. When I feel alone with everything on my plate, the nonstop pushing and pulling for my time, focus, and strength depletes my hope for a better day. That's when I run to You. You know me best. And I know You. Your love, goodness, kindness, and wisdom will always show me who, what, when, where, and why. Your encouragement is such a gift!

**I will find a way to encourage someone
today to honor You.**

The Gift of Friendship

DECEMBER 7

Perfume and incense bring joy to the heart,
and the pleasantness of a friend springs
from their heartfelt advice.
Proverbs 27:9, NIV

All of us have the capacity for mutual esteem. Stronger than an acquaintance, friendship is a special bond you form with someone you trust with yourself. Friends lend a hand, go out of their way to help, rush to your side when needed, and listen with both ears and heart. You could be like Abraham, who was called the friend of God, but that takes time and testing. Perhaps that's true of all friendships. If you need a friend, be a friend.

Thank You, Lord, for the friends You've brought into my life over the decades. My life would be a lot different without these tried-and-true companions. So many have been Your hands and feet to me. Thank You for depositing Your character into them and blessing my life with relationships. During this season of giving, help me to remember them. And, Lord, more than anything, thank You for being my friend.

Bless my friends with more, Lord.

The Lord Bless You

The LORD bless you.
Numbers 6:24, NKJV

In the book of Numbers, the Lord spoke to Moses to tell Aaron, the high priest, and his sons to bless the children of Israel in a specific manner. This particular word for "bless" only occurs fifteen times.[1] The first is the father's blessing from Isaac to Jacob. Other occurrences include caring for strangers, fatherless, and widows, and paying the tithe. The blessing was upon their works and land and always implied an increase. During this season, you have an incredible opportunity to bless others with your prayers.

Father, I thank You for Your many blessings in my life. I receive each one with gratitude in my heart. Today, I want to bring others to Your throne. I stand in the gap for them and ask for forgiveness for anything that might block Your blessing in their lives. I appeal to You now for their sakes and ask for their breakthroughs to victory. May they know their Father's blessing.

The Lord will bless each one I bring to Him today.

The Lord Keep You

DECEMBER 9

The LORD bless you and keep you.
Numbers 6:24, NKJV

This word for "keep" only occurs in this Scripture blessing. It means to watch, preserve, and guard as an overseer.[1] Doesn't that just magnify the Lord's loving care over your life? When you pray this over your dear ones, it invokes His exceptional attention to their needs. Your words are powerful when you place anyone under His keeping and watchful eyes.

Dear Lord, I bring my family, coworkers, neighbors, and all who intersect my life to Your attention today. Be present in their lives. Surround them with protection and guard them against the enemy. Protect their homes, their finances, and their jobs. Set a watch around them. Give a warning when danger is near. For those who don't know You, help them to encounter the one who loves them eternally. Thank You for the precious blood of Your Son, Jesus, who washes our sins away and provides divine protection.

**The Lord will keep, watch, preserve,
and guard all I bring to Him.**

The Lord Shine Upon You

DECEMBER 10

The LORD make His face shine upon you.
Numbers 6:25, NKJV

The Lord always knows where you are and is always with you. But what do you suppose this priestly blessing means? Although we've never seen God, what do you think His face might say when He looks upon you? Is it kind, tender, compassionate, angry, or concerned? The word "shine" means to give or shed light, to be or become light, or to be brightened, illuminated, or enlightened.[1] What a tremendous blessing to be face-to-face with God and become drenched in His light until it fills us to overflowing.

Sometimes, storm clouds of life obscure my vision of You, Lord. I choose to believe You are always shining Your loving face my way. In the morning, I think of You watching over me as I read Your Word. Feeling the wind on my face, I think of You breathing on me. Looking at the stars at night, I think of You looking down on me. You are ever-present in my world.

**The Lord will shine His face on me,
and I will be glad.**

The Lord Be Gracious to You

The LORD make His face shine upon you,
And be gracious to you.
Numbers 6:25, NKJV

This verse is the only time the word "gracious" appears in the Bible. The Hebrew word means to show favor, deal, or grant.[1] Interestingly, its primary root word means to bend down, incline, encamp (like the military), or abide or rest in a tent.[2] Imagine the Lord looking down upon you, reaching for you with His hand, and pulling you to His bosom. Rest there for a moment, and breathe Him in. His gracious love is waiting. Consider how you might do the same for someone in need this season.

Lord, You and I know I try to be gracious with everyone I meet. Sometimes, I fall short but You know that too. With all Your might and power, I am in awe that You care so much about me that You even number the hairs on my head.[3] Receive my thanks for the grace You've poured out on my life. I bless You for all You've done for me.

The Lord is gracious and deserves all my praise.

The Lord's Lift

DECEMBER 12

The LORD lift up His countenance upon you.
Numbers 6:26, NKJV

Interestingly, as in yesterday's verse, the Lord's countenance is similar to shining His face upon you. In this case, the emphasis is on *lift up*, which means to lift, carry, or take up a burden. It can also mean forgive![1] Now, this blessing makes perfect sense. When you draw near to Him and unburden your cares and failures, His face turns to you, shines His light, and lifts burdens up and off. Is there someone you know who needs a lift from you this season?

Lord, I am so grateful for Your forgiving nature. You always look for ways to help me live a life of fullness and abundance. You don't want me to carry burdens that You can so easily lift up and off me. Thank You for always watching over me, wanting to lighten my load. The weight of sin and regret causes me to look down, but You always call me to look up to Your promises.

The Lord will lift up my burdens when I look to Him.

The Lord's Peace

The LORD lift up His countenance
upon you, And give you peace.
Numbers 6:26, NKJV

What is His peace? So much more than your dictionary defines. The word "peace" is *shalom*, and it means completeness, soundness (in body), welfare (in health and prosperity), and peace (from war, but also tranquility and contentment).[1] Digging deeper into its meaning, it means a covenant relationship with God.[2] This blessing surrounds you with all the benefits the Father has for you. What an honor to receive His shalom and bless others with the same.

Oh Father, even during trials, hard decisions, tragedies, and challenges, Your peace is a cherished gift to me. All I need to do is quiet myself, go to my hidden place in You, and breathe You in. You lift my burden, dry my tears, and speak comforting words to my soul. Your shalom opens my thoughts to possibilities. It comforts me in my body, soul, and spirit afflictions. The promises You've given in Your Word are like fire on my lips when I confidently speak them back to You.

The Lord will give me peace in all my circumstances.

The Lord's Name

*So they shall put My name on
the children of Israel, and I will bless them.*
Numbers 6:27, NKJV

The Lord completes His priestly blessing with the order to put His name on the children of Israel. You might think you know what "put" means, but it's so much more than "to place." The Hebrew word certainly means to put, place, or set. But looking deeper, "put" means putting something upon, inserting it into a sheathe, putting it in position, or transforming a thing or person.[1] Think of all the divine names for the Father, Jesus, and Holy Spirit. There are hundreds of divine names that can meet any situation, and you have the privilege of blessing yourself and others with them.

Your name, Lord, invokes power, majesty, promise, answers, and infinitely more than I could ever imagine. During this season, as I prepare to celebrate the gift of Your Son for my life, bring others into my daily prayers. I want to bless them with Your name in their particular situations. Use my prayers to bless them with Your abundance.

**The Lord's name will transform me
and those I pray for.**

I Am Chosen

But you are a chosen people, a royal priesthood,
a holy nation, God's special possession, that you may
declare the praises of him who called you out
of darkness into his wonderful light.
1 Peter 2:9, NIV

Last week, we focused on the Lord's priestly blessing for Aaron and his sons to bless the people. You have the same privilege. God has anointed you with His message and appointed you with His blessing. No matter where you are in life, whether working or retired, single or married, you are chosen to carry His light into a dark world.

I used to think of myself as small and insignificant to the world around me. But, Lord, You've taught me that You care about my every issue. You love to hear my voice, whether it's in praise or prayer. As this year draws to a close, I want to agree with You that I am unique. I am chosen. I carry Your light. And I can still make a difference in my world.

I am chosen to love as God loves me.

I Am Free

DECEMBER 16

When you continue to embrace all that I teach,
you prove that you are my true followers.
For if you embrace the truth, it will release
true freedom into your lives.
John 8:31–32, TPT

Jesus is *the* Word.[1] What would we do without the Word of God and the inspiration we receive from Holy Spirit? Are you embracing all that the Lord has for you, says about you, and desires for you? The truth is that He would have given His life if you were the only person on the earth. There is no lie, no wound, no struggle, and no barrier that can keep you from His love.

Everything changed the day You broke through to my heart, Jesus. I can't imagine my tomorrows without You in them. With every breath and every year left for me on this earth, as I embrace Your truth and live it to its utmost, use me to change lives around me. You've set me free to be all the Father destined me to be.

I am free to live a full and abundant life in the Lord.

I Am Effective

DECEMBER 17

*I pray for you that the faith we share may
effectively deepen your understanding of every good
thing that belongs to you in Christ.*
Philemon 1:6, TPT

You will never be alone in your walk with the Lord. Believers
everywhere seek to find like-minded soldiers of Christ. Whatever
motivation you may feel to serve, teach, share, or encourage is
likely shared by many. You could be the spark that lights the fire in
another. Or perhaps they will see what's hidden in you. It will never
happen unless you let your faith soar to new heights and become the
real *me* you were created to be.

*Once again, Lord, thank You for surrounding me with other saints
whose fellowship stirs and encourages me. They draw me out of my
cocoon and help me spread my wings. Forgive me for my doubts
and unbelief about myself and the good things in me. I'm ready to
be more and do more for the sake of Christ.*

I am an effective saint for the sake of Christ.

I Am His Friend

You are My friends if you do whatever I command you.
John 15:14, NKJV

On Jesus's last night with His disciples, He told them that He no longer called them servants but friends. He affirmed that they knew Him and His teachings and would obey and pass them on. The word "command" may seem intense, but it is a charge that emphasizes the end result or purpose.[1] It reveals where Jesus desires His disciples, others, and you to end up. And that is His friend first and foremost.

As an obedient person raised with shoulds and shouldn'ts, I could easily get caught up in rules, regulations, and duties. But that would not please You, Jesus. You're all about deep and abiding relationships. Let our friendship motivate me in all I set my heart to do, whether in my home, work, church, or public. I commit to listen closely, obey promptly, and follow through with whatever You command.

I am His friend, and I will follow His commands.

I Am Growing

DECEMBER 19

Other seeds *fell into the good soil, and as they*
grew up and increased, they yielded a crop and produced
thirty, sixty, and a hundred times as much.
Mark 4:8, NASB

The Parable of the Sower is probably the most essential teaching Jesus ever gave us. The seed represents the Word of God while the soil represents the condition of the human heart and spirit.[1] Your commitment to this devotional, prayers, and declarations have produced a harvest. You may not see all the growth today, but you are certainly growing in faith and fruitfulness.

Your Word is rich in truth, instruction, and direction. I am comforted by Your promises and inspired by Your encouragement. I want to live a life of abundance—not just in worldly things or wealth but in the prosperity of my soul and spirit. I realize that my life impacts so many. So, what You pour into me, let me pour into others. I'm aiming for a hundredfold, Lord.

I am growing and will produce a
great harvest for my King.

I Am a Runner

Do you not know that in a race all the runners run,
but only one gets the prize? Run in such a way as to get
the prize. Everyone who competes in the games goes into strict
training. They do it to get a crown that will not last,
but we do it to get a crown that will last forever.
1 Corinthians 9:24–25, NIV

Saints may get tired and weary, but they never stop and never give up. You may be midway in your race, but that's where you can gain a second wind. The enemy loves to distract, discourage, and disappoint. But Jesus overcame him, and so will you. Breathe Him in, and finish your race.

As these decades pass, I look to what's ahead, and at times, I get weary, Lord. Sometimes, I wonder if I can handle more challenges and finish this race. But then, there You are on the sideline, rooting me on. I am grateful for Your strength training, Lord. You keep me focused on my eternal prize.

I am a long-distance runner, and I will get my crown.

I Am Fruitful

DECEMBER 21

But the fruit of the Spirit is love, joy, peace,
patience, kindness, goodness, faithfulness, gentleness,
self-control; against such things there is no law.
Galatians 5:22–23, ESV

What do you see when you look in the mirror of your soul? You find it a little uncomfortable if you're like most of us. Why is it that we always seem to judge ourselves more harshly than others? You wonder if you'll ever add up to His perfection. But that's the whole point! You don't have to. He is your perfection, and He's given you His Spirit to help you become more fruitful.

I may be imperfect, but Your Spirit of grace is more than enough to grow me into the woman You designed me to be. Forgive me when I am critical of myself and others, and help me see the progress. I prefer being like You: an encourager rather than a discourager. As I read this list of fruits, Lord, I see improvement in all areas. Thank You for Your Spirit. All I can say is, "More, Lord!"

I am fruitful because He is working His ways in me.

Hear His Whisper

DECEMBER 22

After the earthquake came a fire,
but the LORD was not in the fire.
And after the fire came a gentle whisper.
1 Kings 19:12, NIV

Elijah's story is our story. You may expect to hear the Lord in one way, but He may speak differently. Why is that? He knows what will truly get your attention. As the year draws to a close, ask the Lord for one word for the year ahead. It may come in a flash or quietly drop into your thoughts. Take that one word and study it. Look up its definitions, synonyms, and antonyms. Do a search in your favorite Bible resources for that word or one similar to it. Look up Scriptures and the Hebrew or Greek word meanings. What do you think the Lord is saying? How will you respond to His word to you?

I look forward to Your one word for next year, Lord. I'm intrigued by what You specifically want me to concentrate on. This search will be like a treasure hunt for the Pearl of Great Price.[1]

The Lord will bless me with one word for my new year.

Your Daily Bread

DECEMBER 23

Then the LORD said to Moses, "I will rain down bread from heaven for you. The people are to go out each day and gather enough for that day. In this way I will test them and see whether they will follow my instructions."
Exodus 16:4, NIV

Jesus, the Word of God, is your daily bread. As the year winds down, and you begin to think about what is ahead in the new year, here's a suggestion. Get your daily bread by reading the Word. Whether it's a quiet time in the morning, a coffee break at work, or a just-before-bed refresher, you'll find His Word soothes, instructs, and directs. Try asking the Lord where He wants you to read. If you heard a phrase, a worship song, or a Scripture during the day, then look it up in your free time. Act on these whispers of His Spirit, and get your daily manna.

As the calendar changes, I want to make a change, Lord. I commit to reading Your Word daily and look forward to receiving fresh manna from You.

The Lord will speak to me when I read His Word.

Write It Down

DECEMBER 24

You keep track of all my sorrows.
You have collected all my tears in your bottle.
You have recorded each one in your book.
Psalm 56:8, NLT

Did you know that there are many books in heaven? The Book of Life,[1] the Book of Remembrance,[2] and the Book of Sins.[3] There are hints of others, but they have yet to be explicitly named. As this Scripture states, there's a book that records your tears. Many feel there is a Book of Destiny that lists each person's opportunities while on earth. Consider starting a journal in the new year. The Lord keeps records. Why not you?

Lord, as I begin to journal my thoughts, dreams, and challenges, will You look over my shoulder? When I write, help me to make sense of my life. Speak to me as I seek You. I would cherish your direction for the year ahead.

The Lord will help me fill the pages of my new journal.

Eternal Father

For a Child will be born to us, a Son will be given to us;
And the government will rest on His shoulders;
And His name will be called Wonderful Counselor,
Mighty God, Eternal Father, Prince of Peace.
Isaiah 9:6, NASB

It's here. Christmas is the day we love to celebrate with family. Families all over the world gather in churches to honor the one who gave up everything to become one of us and give us the greatest gift of all: eternal life. Isaiah's prophecy of this child's name should warm your heart, fire your spirit, and bring peace to your soul.

I honor You, Jesus. Today is like no other. It's the day You chose to put on the human condition. You understand stubbed toes, hungry tummies, hurt feelings, and name-calling. You know the taste of salt in tears and the pain of nails driven into Your body. You experienced betrayal, friendship, frustration, and much joy. You came into this world for me. I am forever grateful, my King of kings and Lord of lords.

Lord Jesus, You are my Eternal Father.

Recipes for Life

DECEMBER 26

Surely goodness and mercy shall follow me
all the days of my life, and I shall dwell
in the house of the LORD forever.
Psalm 23:6, ESV

If you don't look back, you'll never see how far you've come. Some say, "Don't look back! Keep pressing. Keep moving." Yes, that's true when you're working toward a goal. But what are you missing when you don't look back? You miss giving praise for answered prayers and progress. Record your needs and those of others on recipe cards and date them. As the year progresses, make up more. When you get an answer, date it and place it in your recipe answer box. At year-end, you'll be glad you did!

Lord, I want more of You and answered prayers in the year ahead. I commit to writing down every need on a recipe card. I will keep them in front of me as a daily reminder that You always listen to me and delight in answering prayers. I want my recipe box filled because of Your goodness and mercy.

My prayers plus Your answers will fill my recipe box.

Prophesy to Your Needs

DECEMBER 27

Then he said to me, "Prophesy over these bones,
and say to them, O dry bones, hear the word of the LORD."
Ezekiel 37:4, ESV

Throughout this year's journey, you've begun your day with a Scripture, the Word of God, and ended the devotion with a prayer and faith-filled declaration. Supernatural life is activated when you apply the Word and His principles to your situation. Ezekiel's Valley of Dry Bones perfectly depicts the Lord's direction. Ezekiel spoke to the dry bones and then to the breath of life, and they became a great army.[1] There's divine power in your words. Speak life!

Your words are life to me, Lord. They bring me hope and wisdom to navigate my physical, emotional, and spiritual life. As I prepare for my new year and all its possibilities, I will stir my faith. May the words I speak call upon You and Your divine power into every situation I bring to Your throne room. Partner with me as I prophesy to my needs and those of others.

I will speak life to every need I bring to the Lord.

See the Good

Who is the person who desires life
And loves length *of days, that he may see good?*
Psalm 34:12, NASB

Dear one, your God sees you, and He sees His good in you. Your struggles, challenges, and efforts to resolve conflict are always under His watchful eyes. He knows your heart and even your heart's desires. You work hard and apply yourself to the best of your ability. As the bridge generation to the aging and the young, you are a key facilitator, caretaker, and mentor. He will always be with you as you are with them.

Thank You, Lord, for the confidence You've built in me over these months. I'm breathing deeper and lighter. You've replaced my worries and weariness with Your promises. I love these opportunities to be real with You as I learn to be the real me You made me to be. I'm learning to love me, live me, and be me and You to others.

I will see my good God in me and through
me all the days of my life.

For the Aging

Even to your old age and gray hairs I am he,
I am he who will sustain you. I have made you and I will
carry you; I will sustain you and I will rescue you.
Isaiah 46:4, NIV

You are the hands and feet of God to those who are aging. You are also His mouthpiece, His prayer warrior, and His earthly partner. Where you go, He goes. You carry His life, His promise, His compassion, and yes, even His energy. The Lord God is your sustainer. When you feel overwhelmed and stretched to the limit, remember He is always with you.

Just as You comfort and care for me, Lord, fill me with compassion
for the elderly. I will one day be their age and need tender loving
care. Help me consider their needs and offer what I have to give.
May I comfort and point them to You as they draw nearer to their
last breath. I know Your heart for widows and widowers. Help me
to grieve with them and point them to You.

I will be patient, loving, and kind
to those who are aging.

For the Young

DECEMBER 30

Through the praise of children and infants
you have established a stronghold against your enemies,
to silence the foe and the avenger.
Psalm 8:2, NIV

As a woman, mother, or grandmother, you have no idea how important you are to the next generation. With the challenges of today's culture, social media distractions, and narratives pushed on our children, they face godless indoctrination. But God. And but you. You play a significant role as a teacher, mentor, and encourager. The Lord entrusts you with their care. Pointing them to God and praise is a powerful weapon. It reminds them to see, believe, thank, pray confidently, and stand tall against the enemy.

Lord, give me opportunities to share my faith with the children
around me. May our interactions be meaningful to them. Help me
to see their potential and foster spiritual growth in creative ways. I
want to impact their lives so that they become strong warriors in
Your kingdom. May Your kingdom come and Your will be done in
their lives.

I will do all I can to help the next generations.

Love into Your Tomorrows

DECEMBER 31

For the entire law is fulfilled in keeping
this one command: "Love your neighbor as yourself."
Galatians 5:14, NIV

You are not under the law but under grace.[1] And His grace is enough to love yourself. That's the whole point of the journey you've been on this year. You've learned to love the *me* God created you to be. And from that place of security, you can love others with God's love. By that expression, you keep His one command.

> *Lord, this is the last day of the year. I look back and see how far I've come into a new relationship with You, myself, and others. Thank You for having faith in me and helping me to have faith in myself. I'm filled with expectation for what next year's journey will be like. I know You are before me, behind me, and around me with Your love. I look forward to applying my one word, reading Your Word daily, keeping a journal, and filing my answered recipe cards. May all of these bless You as they bless me.*

I will love myself, my neighbor, and
my God into my tomorrows.

Notes

WEARY NO MORE

1. See John 10:10.

EARLY RISING

1. "Strong's Hebrew 7836 - shachar - Strong's Exhaustive Concordance." Bible Hub. Accessed March 14, 2024. https://biblehub.com/hebrew/7836.htm.

AM I THIRSTY?

1. See John 4:1–42.

RESPLENDENT

1. "Strong's Hebrew 215 - or - Strong's Concordance." BibleHub.com. Accessed March 5, 2024. https://biblehub.com/hebrew/215.htm.

CHAMPION FRIEND

1. See Genesis 16:13.

LIKE-MINDED

1. See 1 Corinthians 2:16.

UNITED IN LOVE

1. See John 17:22.

ENCOURAGEMENT

1. See 1 Samuel 30:1–20.

THE PRICKLES

1. "Strong's Greek 2759 - kentron - Strong's Concordance." Bible Hub. Accessed March 14, 2024. https://biblehub.com/greek/2759.htm.

TRAUMA FREE

1. See 1 John 4:19.

CONSTRICTION

1. "Strong's Greek 75 - agónizomai - Strong's Concordance." Bible Hub. Accessed March 14, 2024. https://biblehub.com/greek/75.htm.

LIBERATE ME

1. See Luke 6:29.

RENEW

1. "Renew." WordHippo.com. Accessed March 14, 2024. https://www.wordhippo.com/what-is/the-meaning-of-the-word/renew.html.

PRESSING ON

1. See Psalm 139:16.
2. "Strong's Greek 1377 - diókó - Strong's Concordance." BibleHub.com. Accessed March 14, 2024. https://biblehub.com/greek/1377.htm.

STAYING POWER

1. See Mark 9:24.

PAY IT FORWARD

1. See Genesis 18:1; 2 Samuel 9:7; Luke 10:29–37; and John 12:3.

HIS VISION FOR ME

1. "Hebrew 2377 - chazon - Brown-Driver-Briggs 3." BibleHub.com. Accessed May 14, 2024. https://biblehub.com/hebrew/2377.htm.

GOD BLESS AMERICA

1. "America's Covenant with God." 1607Covenant.com. Accessed March 13, 2024. https://1607covenant.com/.

TRAIN UP OUR CHILDREN

1. "United States Committee for UNICEF." Papers of John F Kennedy. Presidential Papers. White House Central Files. Chronological File, Box 11, "July 1963: 16-31." JFK Library. Accessed March 14, 2024. https://www.jfklibrary.org/learn/about-jfk/life-of-john-f-kennedy/john-f-kennedy-quotations#:~:text=%22Children%20are%20the%20world's%20most,Kennedy.

FOR FREEDOM'S SAKE

1. "Death and Dying." Drew Gilpin Faust. National Park Service. Accessed March 8, 2024. https://www.nps.gov/nr/travel/national_cemeteries/death.html.

REST IN PRESENCE

1. See Exodus 33:12–19.

HEART OF THE MATTER

1. "Strong's Hebrew 3820 - leb - Strong's Concordance." BibleHub.com. Accessed March 8, 2024. https://biblehub.com/hebrew/3820.htm.

WINSOME WAYS

1. See 2 Corinthians 3:2.

GRACE TO ENDURE

1. "James 1:4 - Parallel Versions." BibleHub.com. Accessed March 14, 2024. https://biblehub.com/james/1-4.htm.
2. "Strong's Greek 5046 - teleios - Strong's Concordance." BibleHub.com. Accessed March 20, 2024. https://biblehub.com/greek/5046.htm.

COME HOME!

1. See John 14:6.

GIVING HONOR

1. "Hebrew 748 - arak - Brown-Driver-Briggs." BibleHub.com. Accessed March 12, 2024. https://biblehub.com/hebrew/748.htm.

ONE BIG FAMILY

1. See Romans 10:13.

A GIFTED SAINT

1. See Ephesians 4; 1 Corinthians 12; and Romans 12.

SERVE GOD'S PURPOSE

1. "Generation Definition & Usage Examples." Dictionary.com. Accessed March 14, 2024. https://www.dictionary.com/browse/generation.

HIS WORD LIGHTS MY WORLD

1. Recommended resources: BibleHub.com, Google Search, and Wordhippo.com.

STUDY BUDDY

1. I recommend YouVersion on Bible.com.

KINDRED SPIRITS

1. "Strong's Greek 2473 - isopsuchos - HELPS Word Studies." BibleHub.com. Accessed March 9, 2024. https://biblehub.com/greek/2473.htm.

TOGETHER AS ONE

1. See Acts 1:8.

REPLAY AND REPEAT

1. See Deuteronomy 6:5–8.

REMEMBERING

1. "Re-member." Wiktionary.com. Accessed March 9, 2024. https://en.wiktionary.org/wiki/re-member.

ABIDING

1. See John 13–16.

MY FORGIVER

1. "Strong's Greek 3783 - opheiléma - Thayer's Greek Lexicon." BibleHub.com. Accessed March 9, 2024. https://biblehub.com/greek/3783.htm.

MY DELIVERER

1. See Luke 22:32.

BE MAGNIFIED IN ME

1. See Colossians 1:25–28.

KNOW YOUR ENEMY

1. See John 10:1–18.

MY PEACE BOOTS

1. "Army General Orders - US Army Basic." USArmyBasic.com. Accessed March 9, 2024. https://usarmybasic.com/army-knowledge/army-general-orders/.

LORD OF THE HARVEST

1. "Strong's Greek 1189 - deomai - HELPS Word Studies." BibleHub.com. Accessed March 12, 2024. https://biblehub.com/greek/1189.htm.

WAIT FOR HOLY SPIRIT

1. See 1 Corinthians 15:6.

PREPARE IN THE SPIRIT

1. See Deuteronomy 29:4–6 and 18.

PRAYING PRODIGALS HOME

1. See John 16:13, John 6:44; John 14:6; Matthew 13:13–17; Ephesians 3:18; John 3:16; Luke 10:9; Ezekiel 22:30; and James 1:25.

HE IS FAITHFUL

1. See Isaiah 46:10.

A NEW SONG

1. See 2 Corinthians 3:2.

WISE LEADERS

1. See 1 John 5:14–15.

FOR THE CHILDREN'S SAKE

1. See Psalm 115:16.

THANK YOU, YAHWEH-YIREH

1. See Genesis 22:5.

THANK YOU, YAHWEH-SHALOM

1. See Judges 6:1–23.

THANK YOU, YAHWEH-CHEREB

1. See Hebrews 4:12.

THE PROPHETIC GIFT

1. See Luke 21:7–31.
2. See Joel 2:28–29.

THE PASTORAL GIFT

1. See Luke 4:18.

THE NEXT GENERATIONS

1. See Isaiah 60:2; Joel 2:28–29; and Isaiah 54:13.

THE LORD BLESS YOU

1. "yə·ḇā·reḵ·ḵā - Englishman's Concordance." BibleHub.com. Accessed March 9, 2024. https://biblehub.com/hebrew/yevarechcha_1288.htm.

THE LORD KEEP YOU

1. "Strong's Hebrew 8104 - shamar - Strong's Concordance." BibleHub.com. Accessed March 9, 2024. https://biblehub.com/hebrew/8104.htm.

THE LORD SHINE UPON YOU

1. "Strong's Hebrew 215 - or - NAS Exhaustive Concordance." BibleHub.com. Accessed March 5, 2024. https://biblehub.com/hebrew/215.htm.

THE LORD BE GRACIOUS TO YOU

1. "Strong's Hebrew 2603 - chanan - Strong's Exhaustive Concordance." BibleHub.com. Accessed March 9, 2024. https://biblehub.com/hebrew/2603.htm.
2. "Strong's Hebrew 2583 - chanah - NAS Exhaustive Concordance." BibleHub.com. Accessed March 9, 2024. https://biblehub.com/hebrew/2583.htm.
3. See Matthew 10:30.

THE LORD'S LIFT

1. "Strong's Hebrew 5375 - nasa or nasah - NAS Exhaustive Concordance." BibleHub.com. Accessed March 9, 2024. https://biblehub.com/hebrew/5375.htm.

THE LORD'S PEACE

1. "Strong's Hebrew 7965 - shalom - Strong's Concordance." BibleHub.com. Accessed March 9, 2024. https://biblehub.com/hebrew/7965.htm.
2. "Hebrew 7965 - shalom - Brown-Driver-Briggs." BibleHub.com. Accessed March 9, 2024. https://biblehub.com/hebrew/7965.htm.

THE LORD'S NAME

1. "Strong's Hebrew 7760 - sum or sim - Brown-Driver-Briggs." BibleHub.com. Accessed March 9, 2024. https://biblehub.com/hebrew/7760.htm.

I AM FREE

1. See John 1:1–5.

I AM HIS FRIEND

1. "Strong's Greek 1781 - entellomai - Strong's Concordance." BibleHub.com. Accessed March 9, 2024. https://biblehub.com/greek/1781.htm.

I AM GROWING

1. See Mark 4:1–20.

HEAR HIS WHISPER

1. See Matthew 13:45-46.

WRITE IT DOWN

1. See Exodus 32:32 and Revelation 3:5.
2. See Daniel 7:10 and Malachi 3:16.
3. See 2 Corinthians 5:10.

PROPHESY TO YOUR NEEDS

1. See Ezekiel 37:1–14.

LOVE INTO YOUR TOMORROWS

1. See Romans 6:14.

About the Author

Mary Puplava is a daughter, sister, wife, mother of three sons, and grandmother of six. She's now retired from being "The Glue" as webmaster, bookkeeper, human resources and office manager, carpooler, cheerleader, volunteer, pediatric registered occupational therapist, and oldest girl of nine.

At Gathering Place Church, she is a member of the Leadership Team for Visitor Greeting and Growth Track Coordinator, and Prayer Team. She has served on the Women's Council for many years. For several years, she has participated on a daily prayer call and state prayer calls.

Mary spent decades serving others, but her heart was always to write to and for women. She authored a Christian women's newsletter and two blogs that were abandoned due to workload and being called out of retirement for another six years.

She gets you because she's been you. But not anymore. Her prayer vigil and personal journey have prepared her for such a time as this. She caught God's vision of her real *me* and began to live her faith life out loud. She is currently publishing a daily "Today I prayed about…" on social media.

Mary lives in Poway, California, with her husband and their rescue dog, Wellington.

Made in the USA
Columbia, SC
30 October 2024

45293617R10230